D1088916

How Houston Ascended to the Championship in 2022

KINGS OF THE HILL

HOUSTON CHRONICLE

ON THE COVER: Pitcher Cristian Javier, from left, manager Dusty Baker, shortstop Jeremy Peña, pitcher Framber Valdez and catcher Christian Vázquez bask in the glow of the Astros' championship trophy after Game 6 of the World Series at Minute Maid Park.
BRETT COOMER/HOUSTON CHRONICLE

OPPOSITE: A labor dispute that wasn't settled until March 10 forced a week's delay to the 2022 season. After a 5-4 start on the road, the Astros finally played their home opener on April 18 against the Angels, winning 8-3.
BRETT COOMER/HOUSTON CHRONICLE

Copyright © 2022 by Houston Chronicle
All Rights Reserved • ISBN: 978-1-63846-050-3

No part of this book may be reproduced, stored in a retrieval system or transmitted in any form or by any means, electronic, mechanical, photocopying, recording or otherwise, without prior written permission of the copyright owner or the publisher.

This book is an unofficial account of the Astros' 2022 season from news coverage by the Houston Chronicle, and is not endorsed by MLB or the Houston Astros.

Published by Pediment Publishing, a division of
The Pediment Group, Inc. • www.pediment.com
Printed in Canada.

Table of Contents

Credits

Nancy A. Meyer, Publisher and President
Maria Reeve, Editor
Reid Laymance, Sports Editor
Steve Schaeffer, Book Editor/Assistant Sports Editor
Mark Mulligan, Book Photo Editor
Jason Fochtman, Book Photo Editor

Minute Maid
OXY
ASTROS COMMUNITY LEADERS
ConocoPhillips
HALLIBURTON
LEXUS
Schlumberger
reliant
FREEPORT LNG
Methodist
AmegyBank
StubHub
VIVE TU ESTRELLA!
Texas Bay
ULTRA
ROOT 4 THA CHIKIN
Auto Anything
Auto Anything
OPENING DAY
2022

Foreword

As the championship celebration raged on the field at Minute Maid Park, I asked Reggie Jackson, a World Series luminary if ever there were one, his impressions of the 2022 Astros pitching staff.

"I've been wondering," replied Mr. October, now a special adviser to Astros owner Jim Crane, "if this was the best pitching staff I've seen."

From the top of the rotation to the bottom of the bullpen, it was, without question, the best seen in 61 seasons of major league baseball in Houston. And it's why, after a five-year span since the Astros won a championship that would come to be viewed with national scorn, they were on top of the baseball world again.

No championship team is short of magnificent players, and the 2022 Astros were no exception.

Jose Altuve, a second baseman carving out a legitimate case to someday join Jackson in Cooperstown, enjoyed one of his best seasons, matching the 160 OPS+ of his 2017 MVP campaign.

Cuban slugger Yordan Alvarez, with a .306/.406/.613 slash line, cemented his place as one of the game's most fearsome hitters. He further demonstrated this with not one but two "Where were you when he hit that home run?" postseason moments, the first a walk-off missile in the Astros' playoff opener, the second a go-ahead bomb in the World Series clincher.

Kyle Tucker solidified his standing as one of baseball's premier right fielders, pairing 30 homers with 25 stolen bases, reaching 100 RBIs for the first time, and earning his first Gold Glove.

Third baseman Alex Bregman recaptured the form that made him AL MVP runner-up in 2019, producing a line of .294/.379/.569 with three home runs, five doubles and 11 RBIs in 13 postseason games.

And then there was Jeremy Peña. Tasked merely with succeeding the best shortstop the Astros had ever known in Carlos Correa, Peña became the first rookie to win a Gold Glove at the position and made his presence known to the baseball world during a postseason that saw him win MVP honors in the World Series and American League Championship Series.

But truth be told, the 2022 Astros probably wouldn't have become kings of the hill if not for their kings of the hill. Their starting pitchers posted a 2.95 ERA that ranked second in the majors. And the bullpen took a back seat to no one, topping MLB with a cumulative 2.80 ERA.

At the head of the rotation was Justin Verlander, who broke new ground as a 39-year-old ace coming off Tommy John surgery that had shelved him for two seasons. Verlander was merely the best starting pitcher in baseball, compiling an 18-4 record while leading the majors with a 1.75 ERA and 0.83 WHIP.

As the other half of the Killer V's, Frambe[r] Valdez came to define the quality start reeling off 25 in a row to set an MLB single-season record. Like Verlander, Valdez won 2[0] games in the regular season and postseason combined, and the lefthander even became the first Astro to win the All-Star Game.

If opponents thought those two were tough, they really had to cower at th[e] thought of facing Cristian Javier. Among MLB pitchers throwing at least 140 innings Valdez's fellow Dominican was the toughest to hit, limiting those who faced him to a .17[illegible] batting average. And as if throwing the first seven innings of a June no-hitter at Yanke[e] Stadium weren't enough, Javier threw th[e] first six as the Astros no-hit the Phillies in Game 4 of the World Series. Including the playoffs, Javier allowed only eight hits and one run (in an ALDS relief appearance) over his last 35 2/3 innings.

Did we mention the bullpen? Closer Ryan Pressly, who had a regular-season stretch in which he retired a club-record 32 consecutive batters, was lights-out in the playoffs, allowing just six hits, three walks and an unearned run in 11 innings while earning saves in six of his 10 appearances.

Bryan Abreu was no less intimidating. After pitching to a 1.94 ERA in the regular season, he was unscored upon in 10 postseason outings, striking out 19 in 11 1/3 innings while allowing only four hits and four walks.

All told, Astros relievers turned in a 0.83 playoff ERA (five earned runs in 54 1/3 innings), setting a record for any bullpen that threw at least 30 postseason innings.

In only four of their 13 postseason games lid the Astros surrender more than two runs. The Mariners, Yankees and Phillies were hut out once apiece, with Seattle unable o score in an 18-inning marathon. By the ime Valdez turned over a three-run lead to he pen in Game 6 of the World Series, it felt like 30.

Verlander said it well: "What makes this team so great is there's not one particular person that's going to try to go out there and try to be the hero on any given night. We just try to have quality at-bats, try to make quality pitches, try to go to our bullpen with a lead."

The ace could have been speaking of anyone on a roster filled with selfless players. Consider catcher Martín Maldonado, who revealed on the night the Astros won it all that he'd been playing with a sports hernia and broken hand since August. Or Chas McCormick, who, with the Astros clinging to a one-run lead in the ninth inning of World Series Game 5, crashed into the center-field wall at Citizens Bank Park to make what is arguably the greatest catch in franchise history.

Presiding over this remarkable group? Manager Dusty Baker, who in 2020 took over as the right man at the right time.

It's interesting to consider that without the sign-stealing scandal that erupted two years after the Astros won their first title in 2017, Houston never would have needed to hire a replacement for A.J. Hinch. But Baker embraced the chance to manage again and deftly kept the Astros' golden era going, regardless of free-agent losses or opposing fan vitriol. And in his 25th season at the helm of a major league club, he at last got the World Series ring he longed for as a skipper. Baseball indeed works in mysterious ways.

Thanks to the supremely talented and tireless writers and photographers of the Houston Chronicle, this compilation provides a written and pictorial presentation of the Astros' path to their second championship. Included are several stories covering the regular season, as well as accounts from all 13 games of the postseason.

A special shout-out is extended to the Chronicle's Mark Mulligan and Jason Fochtman, who searched through hundreds of images in selecting those found in these commemorative pages. It is hoped fans will find this book a treasured memento they can turn to time and again to relive the highlights that helped make the 2022 Houston Astros what they undisputedly were: kings of the hill.

Steve Schaeffer
Houston Chronicle Assistant Sports Editor
"Kings of the Hill" Book Editor

ASTROS
Minute Maid
2K WINS
OXY
ASTROS COMMUNITY LEADERS
CHEVY
SILVERADO

2,000 man

Dusty Baker reaches a managerial milestone

BY CHANDLER ROME · MAY 3, 2022

Nothing changed on the day Dusty Baker entered a new echelon, more rarefied air for a man who often resides there. He dropped names, dapped up players and did not indulge an inundation of retrospective questions. Baker managed 3,745 regular-season games before this one. If it meant more than others, Baker did not let it show.

Baker projects an air of permanent peace. He is immune to worry and does not dwell on minutiae. The septuagenarian survived a stroke and prostate cancer, lost four managerial jobs, and didn't think he'd ever get a fifth. Spare him any concern about a first baseman with a. 213 batting average.

Yuli Gurriel won the American League batting title months ago. He didn't forget how to hit, but Baker acknowledged his most recent at-bats "are not Yuli-eqsue."

"But what's his name?" Baker wondered with a wide smile. "Yulieski? Yeah, so Yulieski will get Yuli-esque."

Few in baseball carry Baker's cache. He relates to everyone and ostracizes no one. He typifies the term "players' manager," a bilingual Black man who started his career amid segregation and is ending it by restoring respectability.

"Beyond just a manager, he's an amazing person," pitcher Lance McCullers Jr. said. "He helped us through a tough time as a clubhouse in 2020. We were navigating through a lot of choppy water with everything going on, plus COVID. He's earned our respect. It's a big milestone for him."

Turmoil brought Baker to Houston for his "final hurrah." The franchise's search for stability in the wake of a sign-stealing scandal ended with a manager needing one more run at the few milestones still eluding him. Tuesday's 4-0 Astros win over the Mariners fulfilled the first.

During the 24th game of his 25th season, Baker secured the 2,000th win of his magnificent managerial career, cementing him as a near certainty for the Hall of Fame. Baker's wife, Melissa, attended the game along with a litany of friends and family. Baker said he spent the ninth inning talking to those who couldn't — his father, Johnnie Sr.; his mentor, Hank Aaron; and other teammates who've passed away.

"I've been the luckiest person in the whole world to be amongst and in the presence of many greats, on and off the field," Baker said. "I'm probably one of the luckiest men to walk the face of the Earth."

Thanks to Tuesday's victory — a combined four-hitter by Cristian Javier, Blake Taylor, Phil Maton and Bryan Abreu that included home runs by Yordan Alvarez and Jose Altuve — Baker is the 12th manager in major league history to win 2,000 games. Ten of the others are enshrined in Cooperstown. The one who isn't, Bruce Bochy, is not yet eligible for induction.

Tuesday's win left Baker four victories away from passing Bochy on the sport's all-time list. Barring catastrophe, Baker will pass Leo Durocher (2,008) and Walter Alston (2,040) for ninth by season's end.

"I'll get there as long as I live," Baker quipped before the game. "That's my thing. As long as you live and just do your job, I'll get there."

Baker is the first Black manager to reach the 2,000 milestone, another groundbreaking moment for a man with a career full of them. Baker and Los Angeles Dodgers manager Dave Roberts remain baseball's only two Black managers. Baker has long advocated for more participation and inclusion in a sport slow to get it.

"It means extra. It means extra to the culture," Baker said. "It means extra to society. It means extra to my race and extra for, hopefully, others to get the opportunity. And (to) not be the last."

The Astros are Baker's fifth team in a managerial career that almost never arrived. He finished a 19-year playing career in 1986 and never intended to coach. He became a broker but found it did not interest him.

OPPOSITE: The 12th manager to reach 2,000 career victories, Dusty Baker would finish the 2022 season with 2,093, vaulting past Bruce Bochy (2,003), Leo Durocher (2,008) and Walter Alston (2,040) for ninth place all-time. The eight skippers ahead of Baker: Connie Mack (3,731), Tony La Russa (2,902), John McGraw (2,763), Bobby Cox (2,504), Joe Torre (2,326), Sparky Anderson (2,194), Bucky Harris (2,158) and Joe McCarthy (2,125). **KAREN WARREN/HOUSTON CHRONICLE**

RIGHT: Dusty Baker celebrates his milestone victory with Astros owner Jim Crane, who hired him in January 2020 in the wake of the Astros' 2017-18 sign-stealing scandal that resulted in the dismissal of manager A.J. Hinch. **KAREN WARREN/HOUSTON CHRONICLE**

A divorce put his life at a crossroads in the late '80s. Baker prayed about his future and called his father, Johnnie Sr. Father told son he sensed an urge to coach.

Johnnie Sr. told his boy to pray about it. Baker chose Lake Arrowhead in California to consider his options. He checked into a hotel and, as he tells it, received a tap on the shoulder.

"It was Bob Lurie, the owner of the Giants," Baker said. "He said, 'Hey, you need to come join us.' That was my first time there. He told me it was his first time there. If I show up 30 seconds later, I never see him. Or 30 seconds earlier, and he never sees me."

Baker took the turn of events as a sign. His father nudged him along, and Baker accepted San Francisco's offer to coach first base in 1988. He's been on a major league coaching staff for all but two years since.

He won his first game in 1993. He passed Tommy Lasorda, his longtime manager in Los Angeles, with his 1,600th victory in 2013 while with the Cincinnati Reds. Baker mentioned only those two in discussing his most memorable wins.

"I don't look back too much," Baker said. "I probably won't even look forward much. Just get it done and get it out of the way."

Baker managed the Giants for 10 seasons

LEFT: Houston became the fifth managerial home for Dusty Baker, who also managed the San Francisco Giants (1993-2002), Chicago Cubs (2003-06), Cincinnati Reds (2008-13) and Washington Nationals (2016-17). **KAREN WARREN/ HOUSTON CHRONICLE**

before stints with the Chicago Cubs, Reds and Washington Nationals. Baker guided the Giants to a National League pennant in 2002 and posted 840 of his 2,000 wins with them.

The Reds and Nationals both fired Baker after playoff appearances, decisions that irk Baker to this day. After Washington deposed him in 2017, Baker awaited another call. Most presumed he had retired. Baker said nothing of the sort but had resigned himself to his new reality.

"I said, 'Maybe God didn't want me to get it,' " Baker said. "(Then) got the call from (Astros owner) Jim Crane."

Baker's contract expires after this season. He turns 73 in June and, during an introductory news conference three years ago, called the Astros' job his "last hurrah." His future beyond this season is cloudy, but his focus is certain. The 11 other managers with 2,000 wins all have a World Series title. Baker does not.

"I ain't gonna stop. I don't want to stop now," Baker said. "I don't know how long I'm going to manage, but I've always said if I win one, I'm going to win two. I'd hate to be a liar."

60
HOUSTO
SOX
2

Monster mashing

\stros tie major league record with five homers in an inning

3Y CHANDLER ROME · MAY 17, 2022

BOSTON — Maybe the baseballs gained life overnight for a TBS audi-nce. Maybe the Astros found a tell that ipped them off to Nathan Eovaldi's pitch equencing. Maybe Houston's lineup, limited or some of this season and languishing for nuch of the rest, reverted to a form so many resumed it would take. Maybe a group of ood hitters entered with a foolproof plan nd simply solved one of Boston's best start-ng pitchers.

Rational reasons for a record-setting night lo exist, but some events just defy expla-ation. On Tuesday night at Fenway Park, place steeped in more history than most f its 29 counterparts, the Astros authored nother piece of it.

For more than 20 minutes, a group of nine Iouston hitters morphed into something uperhuman, delivering a brand of offensive aseball many presumed impossible in the port's current state. They matched a major eague record with five home runs in the econd inning of a 13-4 win, bringing the port back to a bygone era.

"There is no explanation. Sometimes you it the great ones good; sometimes the so-so nes, you don't hit them," manager Dusty 3aker said. "There's not an explanation for verything. In batting practice, you can't hit hat many home runs. It's true. It's not that asy to hit home runs. It was just our day."

Houston is the eighth team in major league history to hit five home runs in an inning and the first since the 2020 New York Yankees. Four of the other occurrences came before 1966.

"I don't think I've ever seen that before," said Baker, a 73-year-old lifer with more games forgotten than most remember. "I've had some good teams, played on some good teams, but that was a first right there."

Players around the sport, including some inside the Astros' clubhouse, have privately excoriated inconsistencies they perceive with the baseballs. They are not traveling like they did two, three or four years ago. New York Mets hitting coach Eric Chavez suggested last month the sport is juicing balls for games airing on national television.

No one in the Astros' clubhouse has shared such a conspiracy. Watching the lineup per-form suggests any baseball design flaw is an annoyance, not a disadvantage. The lineup entered Tuesday's game with 49 home runs. Only the New York Yankees had more.

Houston employs a slew of sluggers. One will contend for the league's home run ti-tle. Another has American League Most Valuable Player aspirations. Another is asserting himself as a favorite for American League Rookie of the Year.

The three men teamed to catalyze a sec-ond-inning ambush of Eovaldi. Boston's starter needed five pitches to dispatch Houston during the first inning. Yordan Alvarez saw three pitches in the second before he pounced.

On the fourth offering, Alvarez dropped his barrel on a four-seam fastball on the outer half. The baseball traveled where few lefthanded hitters can direct it, atop the Green Monster seats in left field for a solo home run.

Alvarez's 12th home run of the season left him two shy of Aaron Judge for the major league lead. It began a bludgeoning of Eovaldi, an Alvin product who will want to forget everything about this Texas-sized tattooing.

Eovaldi fired 34 pitches in the second in-ning. Houston struck eight of them for hits. Five left the ballpark, and another created a milestone. Jose Altuve's first-pitch double down the third-base line gave him 1,800 career hits. Only 10 active players have more. He is the fourth man in Astros history to cross the threshold, a seismic step on the daunting journey toward 3,000.

Tuesday's triumphs made Altuve's ac-complishments a mere footnote. The lineup matched its season high with 13 runs and 15 hits. Kyle Tucker hit two home runs, includ-ing a fourth-inning grand slam. Tucker had six RBIs by the fourth inning.

Jeremy Peña, Houston's precocious rookie who grew up an hour from Fenway Park, fulfilled his boyhood fantasy. He called it a "dream come true" to play in these hallowed

OPPOSITE: To the dismay of Red Sox third baseman Rafael Devers, Michael Brantley heads for the plate after hitting the Astros' fourth of five second-inning home runs off Nathan Eovaldi. Brantley's fourth Astros season would consist of only 64 games, over which he hit .288. On June 28, he went on the injured list with a shoulder ailment that turned out to be season-ending.
DAVID BUTLER II/USA TODAY SPORTS

RIGHT: Yuli Gurriel, whose single followed Yordan Alvarez's home run leading off the second, comes home after the next batter, Kyle Tucker (background), went deep. Gurriel would bat again in the inning, completing the seven-run uprising with the Astros' fifth homer of the frame, which tied a major league record previously accomplished seven times.
DAVID BUTLER II/USA TODAY SPORTS

grounds. After four days away due to a knee injury, he received his wish. On Monday, Peña signed his name inside the Green Monster alongside those of thousands of players, staff and baseball lifers who make their first trip here.

A night later, he parked the second pitch he saw atop it. Peña's sprint around the bases seemed faster than any in recent memory.

Peña's parents and a group of around 50 friends watched him round the bases and actualize his dream. His stoicism is lauded, but even he could not contain the joy simmering inside. Peña perpetually preaches he's only here to help the team win games. Tuesday furthered the objective.

Eovaldi entered the evening among the sport's elite. He exited as a trivia answer for Houston baseball fans forever. The Astros inflicted upon him the sort of beating few starting pitchers have ever experienced. Just two other pitchers in major league history had ever surrendered five home runs in an inning — Chase Anderson (2020) and Michae Blazek (2017).

Both men ended their careers with a ERA north of 4.20. Eovaldi garnered a All-Star appearance last season. He finishe fourth in American League Cy Young voting. The Astros did not attack some scrul summoned from the minor leagues. The humiliated a man with an ace-caliber arsenal a four-seam fastball that can reach 98 mp

LEFT: As if his participation in the Astros' five-homer second inning weren't enough, Kyle Tucker (30) hit a grand slam in the fourth off Boston reliever Tyler Danish. Celebrating with Tucker are Yordan Alvarez (44), Jose Siri (26) and Yuli Gurriel.
DAVID BUTLER II/USA TODAY SPORTS

aired with four off-speed pitches designed ɔ keep elite lineups guessing. The Astros ad every answer.

Houston's home runs arrived on three eparate pitch types. Alvarez and Tucker truck four-seam fastballs. Peña jumped on poorly executed cutter, completing a back-ɔ-back effort with Tucker. Four batters later, Michael Brantley bludgeoned a cutter 405 eet away into the right-field seats.

"When our guys swing at strikes and they feel good," hitting coach Troy Snitker said, "I know they don't think anybody can get them out."

Eovaldi procured two outs in the frame. Jose Siri flew out for the first, but it lent only a momentary reprieve. Nine-hole hitter Martín Maldonado singled, and Altuve rolled his historic double down the left-field line, allowing the middle of this order another look at Eovaldi.

Brantley and Yuli Gurriel saw three pitches apiece. Gurriel completed the carnage by crushing a curveball into the second row of Green Monster seats, sending Alex Cora from the dugout to fetch his starter and decipher how this all happened.

"You can't explain it," Snitker said. "We just got hot. It happened fast. You don't know when stuff like that is coming. Our guys are really good. They can explode at any moment, and you just enjoy it.

STROS
77

9 Pitches, 3 strikeouts – twice!

Luis Garcia, Phil Maton become first pair to throw immaculate inning in same game

BY CHANDLER ROME · JUNE 15, 2022

ARLINGTON — The improbable became imminent, and so few watching knew how to react. The manager who has seen everything never witnessed this. Somewhere inside the third-base dugout sat the starting pitcher, his day of work complete and a milestone achieved. Luis Garcia now devoted himself to casual conversation while history happened in front of him.

The voice inside Phil Maton's cap called for a fastball. Anxiety attempted to overtake one of the Astros' most stoic relievers. He started the seventh inning with six straight four-seamers, secured two strikeouts, and became aware of the moment. Immaculate innings are more than infrequent. Only 104 had ever been thrown in modern major league history.

Maton never pitched one. Not as a Little Leaguer or Louisiana Tech standout and certainly not at any point in his seven-year professional career. One wondered whether he had ever witnessed the pinnacle of pitching: three strikeouts on nine pitches.

"Yeah," Maton said, "in the second inning today."

No game in major league history had ever featured two immaculate innings. The Astros threw two during Wednesday's 9-2 win over the Rangers. Both arrived against the same three Texas batters, a piece of baseball history established in almost unfathomable fashion.

"Pretty damn cool," pitching coach Josh Miller said. "It's not something you set out to really do. It's a product of executing and making good pitches. Once you get the first two strikeouts of an inning on six pitches, you're like 'Aaaaallll right, let's see what happens.' It was neat to follow along."

There had never been two immaculate innings on one calendar date, let alone in one game. Yet during a mundane matinee between two intrastate rivals, Garcia struck out Rangers hitters Nathaniel Lowe, Ezequiel Duran and Brad Miller on nine pitches during the second inning. Maton managed to replicate it in the seventh.

Houston had seven immaculate innings in franchise history entering the game — six as the Astros and another from its days as the Colt .45s. Will Harris threw the last one on Sept. 27, 2019, against the Angels.

"To be a part of that and know that you made history, that's something that any player is proud of," catcher Martín Maldonado said. "I'm glad I was the catcher in that situation."

Lowe, Duran and Miller hit sixth, seventh and eighth in Texas' order. Garcia generated swinging strikeouts from all three during a bounce-back second inning.

The Astros' lineup hit for 28 minutes and scored six times in the top of the first, more runs than they scored in 48 other games this season. Texas made a pitching change midway through the frame, forcing Garcia to wait more than 40 minutes from the time he finished pregame warmups to when he arrived for his first pitch.

"I'm not going to tell the guys to stop scoring runs — that's a good thing — but he did the best he could," Josh Miller said. "He went and threw some in the cage and did his normal routine otherwise, but he did look like a different guy after that first inning."

Garcia required 30 pitches to escape a plodding first frame. He surrendered an unearned run but protected the lead with which he entered.

Garcia eschewed his four-seam fastball in favor of his three secondary offerings during the second. Lowe tried to bunt against Houston's defensive shift to start the frame. He fouled the pitch instead. Garcia generated five foul balls during the inning. Lowe had two of them before waving over a two-strike cutter, Garcia's trademark pitch.

Duran swung through a first-pitch cutter before seeing consecutive sliders. He foul-tipped the second one into Maldonado's mitt, permitting Garcia to defy convention and consider the stakes.

On May 29, Garcia carried a no-hitter into the sixth inning against the Seattle Mariners. The righthander remarked afterward he didn't think about it because "every time you think like that, s--- happens." Luis Torrens lined a single into left field to spoil the bid, perhaps bolstering Garcia's claim.

"This time," Garcia said Wednesday, "I

OPPOSITE: Astros righthander Luis Garcia, who in 2021 was runner-up for American League Rookie of the Year, made quick work of the Rangers' Nathaniel Lowe, Ezequiel Duran and Brad Miller, striking them out on nine pitches in the second inning. **JEROME MIRON/USA TODAY SPORTS**

RIGHT: After the eighth immaculate inning in franchise history had been thrown five frames earlier, Astros reliever Phil Maton made it nine in the seventh, victimizing the same three Texas hitters: Nathaniel Lowe, Ezequiel Duran and Brad Miller. The other Houston pitchers to accomplish the feat before Maton and Luis Garcia were Bob Bruce (1964), Pete Harnisch (1991), Mike Magnante (1997), Randy Johnson (1998), Shane Reynolds (1999), Brandon Backe (2004) and Will Harris (2019).
JEROME MIRON/USA TODAY SPORTS

thought about it. Let's go for it. And I'm glad that it happened."

Miller fouled off a changeup and curveball before Garcia got him to swing over another darting cutter. Josh Miller retrieved the baseball and had it authenticated. Garcia had it on display in Houston's celebratory postgame clubhouse.

"It was great. It is a great achievement," said Garcia, who reminded reporters he threw an immaculate inning in Grapefruit League play last year.

"But this counts. I'm glad for that."

Garcia struck out Leody Taveras on three pitches to start the third, giving him four consecutive punchouts on 12 pitches. A first-pitch ball to Marcus Semien ended the stunning string of dominance.

Corey Seager struck a solo homer for the only other damage against Garcia. He gave way to Maton after striking out nine across six innings of two-run ball.

Maton, the trade deadline acquisition who dominated during Houston's World Series run last season, arrived in search of some continuity. He brought a 3.46 ERA and 1.31 WHIP into his appearance.

OPPOSITE: Phil Maton, acquired from Cleveland in July 2021, had a big bullpen role as the Astros went on to that year's World Series. But he didn't participate in the 2022 postseason after breaking a bone in his right hand. The injury occurred when Maton, dissatisfied with his performance in the regular-season finale against Philadelphia, punched his locker. In that game, Maton collected only one out while surrendering two earned runs and two hits — including one to his younger brother, Nick, a utility man for the Phillies.
JEROME MIRON/USA TODAY SPORTS

Maton lowered both by bullying the same trio Garcia tamed. He threw nine straight four-seam fastballs ranging from 90.8 to 91.9 mph. Lowe swung through the first one and foul-tipped the next two. Duran sandwiched a foul tip around two called strikes, bringing Brad Miller to bat as the team's final hope.

"I was starting to get a little anxious because Maldy kept calling fastballs," Maton said. "Ultimately, I just kind of stuck with his game plan in that situation and just kept throwing them."

Miller swung through all three of Maton's offerings. The oft-stoic reliever sauntered from the mound while Houston's dugout devolved into delirium. Maldonado mistakenly threw the final ball to Alex Bregman — common after inning-ending strikeouts. Bregman often tosses it to fans.

Josh Miller had to make sure the keepsake stayed in the ballpark. Too enthralled in his conversation, Garcia had to ask teammates what happened.

"That feels so good. It's history," Garcia said. "I'm so happy for me and for Phil. I don't know what to say. I'm just happy."

53
NIKE
NIKE

Can't touch this

Why 'El Reptil?' Cristian Javier demonstrates in combined no-hitter at Yankee Stadium

BY CHANDLER ROME · JUNE 25, 2022

NEW YORK — They call Cristian Javier "El Reptil" for the manner in which he works. He is methodical and meticulous and exudes almost no outward emotion. Those not aware he's around will assume he's absent. Snakes slither unseen and strike when few expect it. Javier says nothing, shows a soft smile, and can sneak up on a sport that now realizes his potential.

On a sun-splashed Saturday afternoon, Javier introduced himself to the baseball world on one of the game's hallowed stages. He awoke as the sixth starter in a stacked starting rotation, a $10,000 international signee with potential the Astros had not consistently harnessed. He exited with an eternal place in Houston baseball history.

Javier bullied baseball's best lineup for seven hitless innings, stealing any spotlight the New York Yankees hoped this four-game series would afford them. Relievers Héctor Neris and Ryan Pressly procured the final six outs, after which Houston's dugout spilled onto the field in a frenzy.

The trio teamed to throw the 14th no-hitter in Astros history during a 3-0 win at Yankee Stadium.

The Yankees had not been the victims of a no-hitter since six Astros hurlers teamed to throw one on June 11, 2003, at the original Yankee Stadium. Javier, Neris and Pressly produced the first no-hitter in 13 seasons inside the new ballpark, where a near-capacity crowd of more than 45,000 watched in stunned silence.

"We love this atmosphere," catcher Martín Maldonado said. "We love games like this. ... It was a big series. A lot of people are talking about the Yankees, and they don't talk much (about) the Astros. I feel we are still the same team. We love competing out there, and we felt like it was a playoff game coming into the series."

Justin Verlander threw the Astros' last no-hitter on Sept. 1, 2019, against the Toronto Blue Jays. Javier had no chance to complete his masterpiece alone.

Verlander is an established ace without any doubts about his workload. Javier is a promising 25-year-old with only 211 innings of major league experience. He made 28 major league starts before Saturday. Only once did he exceed 100 pitches. Overtaxing his arm in pursuit of personal achievement is a choice the Astros refused to make. That they even allowed him to throw 115 felt aggressive.

"He was the best version of himself," pitching coach Josh Miller said. "Threw strike one a bunch, had the good slider going. His fastball command was pretty good. It's just a unique look for lineups, and it showed today."

Javier surpassed any rational expectation the Astros harbored before the game. When the starting rotation is at full health, Javier is its seventh starter. He brought a 3.07 ERA and 1.17 WHIP to the ballpark. He had not pitched into the seventh inning all season.

Javier relies on a high-spin four-seam fastball without overwhelming velocity. He is a fly ball pitcher who is difficult to hit — opponents had a .208 average against him entering Saturday — but sometimes undone by bouts of inconsistent command. He walked 4.7 batters per nine innings last season and 3.7 per nine in the 13 appearances preceding this one.

Lineups that fancy themselves the sport's best should exploit such pitchers. The Yankees lead the majors in home runs, OPS and OPS+. Presumptive American League MVP Aaron Judge sits atop their batting order. His 27 home runs are the most in the majors. The three men slotted behind Judge on Saturday — Anthony Rizzo, Josh Donaldson and Giancarlo Stanton — have combined for five Silver Sluggers, 10 All-Star appearances and two MVP awards.

Javier held the foursome hitless in 12 plate appearances. Seven of them ended in strikeouts. Javier struck out a career-high 13 batters. Donaldson got on base twice against him, walking in the first following a questionable check-swing call and reaching on Alex Bregman's throwing error in the seventh. No other New York hitter reached.

Judge and Stanton teamed to strike out

OPPOSITE: In his seven no-hit innings against the Yankees, Astros righthander Cristian Javier walked one batter, Josh Donaldson, who also reached on an error. Additionally, Javier struck out 13 batters, a career high he topped in his next start on July 1, when he fanned 14 Los Angeles Angels at Minute Maid Park.
JESSICA ALCHEH/USA TODAY SPORTS

RIGHT: The Astros celebrate the first no-hitter in the 14-season history of the new Yankee Stadium. New York hadn't been no-hit since 2003, when six Astros pitchers — Roy Oswalt, Peter Munro, Kirk Saarloos, Brad Lidge, Octavio Dotal and Billy Wagner — combined for one at the original Yankee Stadium.
JESSICA ALCHEH/USA TODAY SPORTS

five times while Javier worked. The Yankees took 56 swings against him and whiffed 20 times. Javier's slider played perfectly against New York's righthanded-heavy batting order. He stayed ahead in the count, crucial for a pitcher who rarely does it.

Javier entered the outing throwing first-pitch strikes just 50.6 percent of the time. None of the 111 qualified major league pitchers had a lower rate. Falling behind against this Yankees lineup is a fatal mistake. Javier avoided it. Javier threw a first-pitch strike to 12 of the 23 hitters he saw. The Yankees could not square up his high-spin fastball, thrown harder and with better command than Javier had managed all season.

"I noticed in the throwing program earlier in the week, the pitches were doing what they were supposed to," Javier said through an interpreter. "Also, in the bullpen today before the game, pitches were doing what I wanted them to do. I went out there and asked God to give me strength and help me. Thankfully, I was able to have a good game today."

Javier averaged 94.6 mph on the 79 four-seamers he threw, a full mile per hour above his yearlong normal. New York put just nine balls in play against him. Only one exited a bat harder than 100 mph — a fifth-inning fly out from Gleyber Torres that traveled 297 feet. Most no-hitters require at least one remarkable defensive play. Javier needed none.

"He was masterful," manager Dusty Baker said. "He's a pretty cool player to be so young. He doesn't show very much emotion. He trains hard, works hard. He's just an outstanding young man."

After Donaldson drew the dubious first-inning walk, Javier retired the next 16 New York hitters he saw. He matched zeros with Gerrit Cole, the former Astros superstar who signed a $324 million free-agent deal to become the ace of his favorite team from boyhood.

Cole carved up the Astros across seven spectacular innings. Rookie J.J. Matijevic mashed his only mistake for a solo home run in the seventh. Cole let a 99.7 mph four-seamer leak too far inside. Matijevic struck it 403 feet into the second deck of right-field seats, affording Javier the only run of support he required.

"He's a young guy, but he looks like he could be good for a long time in the game," Neris said of his starter. "When he focuses and hits the spots he wants, the pitches he

LEFT: The 14th no-hitter in Houston franchise history was a team effort by, from left, closer Ryan Pressly, catcher Martín Maldonado, setup man Héctor Neris and starter Cristian Javier. The previous 13 were thrown by Justin Verlander (2019), Aaron Sanchez/Will Harris/Joe Biagini/Chris Devenski (2019), Mike Fiers (2015), Roy Oswalt/Peter Munro/Kirk Saarloos/Brad Lidge/Octavio Dotel/Billy Wagner (2003), Darryl Kile (1993), Mike Scott (1986), Nolan Ryan (1981), Ken Forsch (1979), Larry Dierker (1976), Don Wilson (1969 and 1967), Ken Johnson (1964, in a 1-0 loss to the Reds) and Don Nottebart (1963).
JESSICA ALCHEH/USA TODAY SPORTS

has are good enough to be great for a long time here."

Neris began to toss in Houston's bullpen before the seventh inning began. Baker conferred with Miller to establish a limit for Javier's outing. He needed 91 pitches to finish six frames. He had not thrown more than 96 all season.

"I was aware that the no-hitter was going on, but in between innings I was trying to stay focused and stay calm," Javier said. "I just tried to stay focused every single pitch in the game. Even in the dugout, the guys didn't go near me, and I didn't go near them, either. I just tried to stay focused the whole time."

Baker and Miller set 100 pitches as something of a soft limit, but both had to be mindful of a game still in the balance. Houston led just 1-0 when Javier sauntered out for the seventh. One mistake would not only wreck the bid for history but also a game Houston needed to win.

Neris began to loosen in the bullpen before Javier faced a hitter. Rizzo worked him for eight pitches before swinging through a full-count four-seamer. Thirteen of Javier's 20 whiffs arrived against it.

Donaldson followed and put one in play. Bregman fielded the bouncer but sailed the throw to first base. The gaffe allowed Stanton and Torres two chances to save their team from embarrassment. Javier's pitch count reached 104, three shy of his career high. Baker and Miller allowed him to continue.

"We were just kind of trying to win the game," Miller said. "He looked strong. Didn't see a trail-off with his stuff in the sixth or seventh inning. We were going to roll with him."

Javier maintained his velocity throughout a frame few thought he'd see. He fired 11 pitches to Stanton and Torres. Five arrived harder than 94 mph. Stanton watched one paint the outside corner for a crucial second strikeout.

Torres watched another sail high and almost elude Maldonado in a 2-2 count. Miller had determined Torres as Javier's last hitter regardless of the result. He spun a full-count slider that seemed to back up. Torres swung right through it.

Javier leapt from the mound and allowed himself a moment of celebration. He pumped his fists and let out one yell before approaching the foul line. He made the sign of the cross, and *El Reptil*'s face turned back to stone.

Mind over batter

Framber Valdez becomes first Astros pitcher to get an All-Star Game win

BY CHANDLER ROME • JULY 19, 2022

LOS ANGELES — He looked nothing like the lefthander the Astros took a $10,000 chance on in 2015 or the erratic southpaw stowed in the back of a bullpen in hopes he'd never actually be called upon. Framber Valdez is rewriting every narrative surrounding him, one darting sinker or devastating curveball at a time. He mellowed his mind, reestablished his focus and found himself on one of the biggest stages baseball can offer.

"It's one of those things where we have goals, and sometimes you reach that goal," Valdez said through an interpreter. "Sometimes you don't. To be here at the All-Star Game, get the win, it's one of those things I just say wow. A dream come true."

In an exhibition involving players with far greater pedigree, Valdez became the first pitcher in Houston franchise history to win the All-Star Game. The Astros had 38 other All-Star appearances by a pitcher prior to Valdez's perfect third inning during Tuesday's 3-2 American League win. Nolan Ryan and Roy Oswalt combined for four of them. Roger Clemens and Justin Verlander each made one apiece.

None can claim what Valdez captured during an 11-pitch third inning. It offered a snapshot of all that makes Valdez so menacing — and the strides he's made to control it.

A stage like Tuesday's once felt too big for Valdez to handle. Counsel from Astros sports psychologist Dr. Andy Nuñez has changed that. The two talk before each of Valdez's outings. Before Tuesday, Nuñez wrote him this: "If you have peace, you will have balance; if you have balance, you will have control; if you have control, then you will be able to do everything."

Manager Dusty Baker always planned to pitch Valdez in the third inning. Juan Soto, Manny Machado and Freddie Freeman loomed to face him. The three men have combined for six Silver Sluggers and 14 All-Star appearances. Valdez did not seem unnerved for a man making his first. He touched 96 mph and averaged 95.1 mph with his sinker — more than a mile per hour above his season average.

"I wasn't nervous. I was really excited," Valdez said. "I had to calm myself down, had to breathe a little bit and remind myself it's the same game — it's still a baseball game I'm playing — and I was able to get it done."

Valdez needed to stabilize a shaky start from the American League. Starter Shane McClanahan issued two first-inning runs. Leadoff man Shohei Ohtani started the game with a single but got picked off first base by starter Clayton Kershaw. The AL mustered one other baserunner before Valdez entered.

The southpaw fell behind all three batters he faced. Valdez threw just six of his 11 pitches for strikes and did not once spin his trademark curveball. It did not matter.

Valdez's sinker is one of the sport's most difficult pitches to elevate. He induces ground balls at a 67.2 percent clip. No other qualified starter generates them more than 57 percent of the time.

Better command of the pitch has morphed Valdez into something more than just the curveball artist the sport once thought he was. He can flash a changeup or mix in an occasional four-seamer, and this past winter, he added a cutter as another weapon against lefthanded hitters.

"I thought if I do get a lefty up there, I was going to throw that cutter a little bit more," Valdez said.

Two of the three hitters he faced Tuesday hit lefthanded. Valdez threw four cutters as a result. Soto saw three of them. The final one slipped from Valdez's left hand and sailed inside against Soto. Soto playfully acted as if he'd charge the mound. Valdez waved his glove as if to welcome a tussle with his fellow Dominican.

"We were just kidding around," Valdez said. "He kept telling me, 'Throw a fastball, throw a fastball.' I said, 'Well, I've been throwing a lot of fastballs.' "

Soto fouled a sinker before chopping another into a defense perfectly positioned against him. The American League deployed a drastic pull shift against Washington's lefthanded-hitting slugger. Soto's ground ball traveled straight to second baseman Andrés Giménez in shallow right field.

OPPOSITE: In his third-inning All-Star Game stint for the American League, Framber Valdez retired the side 1-2-3, inducing bounce outs from Juan Soto and Manny Machado and a fly out by Freddie Freeman. At season's end, Valdez would have a 17-6 record and 2.82 ERA after pitching an AL-leading 201 1/3 innings. He also would own a single-season major league record of 25 consecutive quality starts.

ROBERT HANASHIRO/USA TODAY SPORTS

RIGHT: Astros skipper Dusty Baker, who by virtue of Houston's 2021 pennant got to manage the American League, came out a 3-2 All-Star Game winner thanks to fourth-inning home runs by the Yankees' Giancarlo Stanton and Twins' Byron Buxton.
JAYNE KAMIN-ONCEA/USA TODAY SPORTS

Soto and Machado both bounced out against Valdez's patented sinker. Valdez threw six sinkers, four cutters and one four-seam fastball during his appearance. The scoreless frame allowed the AL's star-studded lineup to turn over. Two of its most famous sluggers rewarded the effort.

Giancarlo Stanton and Byron Buxton unleashed back-to-back home runs against Dodgers righthander Tony Gonsolin, putting Valdez in position for the victory. Stanton's two-run blast traveled 457 feet and earned him Most Valuable Player honors. Buxton's go-ahead solo shot landed in the National League bullpen.

Stanton and Buxton swatted the first back-to-back home runs in an All-Star Game since 2018, when Astros teammates Alex Bregman and George Springer struck them against Ross Stripling — another Dodgers hurler. Bregman captured Most Valuable Player honors after hitting his shot, becoming the first man in Astros history to earn the award.

Valdez etched his name alongside him Tuesday. Before he could, one final task loomed. Freeman emerged from the dugout to pinch-hit. A roar from his home Dodger Stadium crowd accompanied it. They chanted "Fred-die, Fred-die" as he stepped in to see Valdez, against whom he struck a home run during the 2021 World Series.

"When I went out there, I just said, 'I'm going to throw my best pitch, my sinker,' " Valdez said.

Valdez threw two of them. Freeman flared the second into shallow right field, again into

LEFT: Hours before pitching at Dodger Stadium in the 92nd Midsummer Classic, Framber Valdez rocked the Red Carpet Show at L.A. Live.
GARY A. VASQUEZ/USA TODAY SPORTS

the shift. Giménez stood in perfect position. He gloved the baseball, threw to first and sent Valdez off with a smile.

Most All-Stars exit the dugout and head home after they are pulled. This is, after all, an All-Star break. Any rest and relaxation is valued after two dizzying days at the Midsummer Classic.

Valdez bucked the trend. The first-time All-Star remained in the first-base dugout for the final six innings. He chopped it up with rivals and made new friends as eight more American League pitchers preserved his victory.

"I thought it was kind of like the regular season, where you have to go through the fourth or fifth or something like that," Valdez said. "But once I came out and heard I could be the winner, I was really happy."

Inside the visitors' clubhouse, a reporter informed Valdez he made Astros history. Lockermate Kyle Tucker raised his eyebrows and offered congratulations. Valdez wore a smile that no one could wipe off. The difference in him is almost impossible to describe, down to the dreadlocks he got in preparation for this appearance — one that allowed a nation a look at a reinvented man.

"It helped me a lot," Valdez said with a smile so wide it became hard to decipher words. "I feel really good. I got style. I got some flow going, so that helped me a lot.

"Obviously, it was good just to be here at the All-Star Game, but to get the win, I'm just glad for all the work I put in and for all that's coming out of it."

ARCIA
77
HOUS

21-run salute

Alex Bregman gets inside White Sox's heads, helps Astros tie team record with 25 hits

BY CHANDLER ROME · AUG. 18, 2022

CHICAGO — Power and paranoia are fueling Alex Bregman's ascension back into a force. August has morphed him into baseball's most balked about player, a poster child for baserunners' clandestine practices behind the pitcher's mound. Teams seem in constant fear Bregman will reach second base, peek inside their gloves and relay home what he sees.

Pitchers have two options for recourse: protect themselves or prevent Bregman from touching second. Both appear impossible. Bregman is tormenting teams with both bat and brain while authoring one of his best months of the past three years. A search for the 2019 version of Bregman has stopped this August.

"I know everybody always says 2018 or 2019, but I think each year is different," Bregman said. "Definitely, I'm trying to get back to the mechanics I had those two years, because the previous two, mechanically, I wasn't the same.

"My front hip was wide open, and it was making me spin and kind of cut the baseball instead of staying through it and be able to drive it. We've been working hard at it this year."

Bregman drove in a career-high six runs and collected four extra-base hits Thursday during the Astros' 21-5 destruction of the Chicago White Sox at Guaranteed Rate Field. Bregman now has 12 extra-base hits in 58 August at-bats. His sixth career four-hit game helped to catalyze one of Houston's most complete offensive outputs in years. Ten Astros finished with at least one hit. Seven starters had multi-hit games.

"We made a statement," outfielder Chas McCormick said. "We have a good offense."

Houston matched a franchise record with 25 hits and finished two runs shy of matching a club mark. Bregman, Kyle Tucker and Christian Vázquez all had four-hit games. McCormick had a three-hit afternoon and drove in five runs. White Sox second baseman Josh Harrison surrendered the Astros' final six hits and four runs while pitching the ninth inning.

"I think guys did a really good job of not giving any at-bats away," Bregman said. "It's August. It's late in the year, but the guys' focus was really good today. We swung at good pitches to hit, and I was proud of our at-bats today as a unit."

Bregman struck two home runs in a game for the first time since May 28, 2019. Five of his 20 homers have arrived during the first 18 days of August, a span in which he's driven the ball with more authority than at any previous point this season.

Bregman boasts a career .499 slugging percentage. On the Fourth of July, after 76 games and 266 at-bats, it sat at .399. Bregman flew open in his batting stance far too often and pulled off the baseball. Landing closed allows Bregman to stay through pitches and hit line drives toward the middle of the field.

"The last few years mechanically, I haven't been where I wanted to be," Bregman said. "I've really been just working hard in the cage every single day, beating it into my head that I need to stay closed, stay closed, stay closed with every swing that I take. Today was better. Today was a really good day of executing mechanics."

Bregman is now slugging .472. Since Aug. 1, his OPS has ballooned from .773 to .839, trailing only Yordan Alvarez and Jose Altuve for the team lead. Twenty-five of Bregman's last 47 hits have garnered extra bases.

Four of them arrived Thursday. Both of his home runs came against former Astros farmhand Vince Velasquez, prolonging a farce Lucas Giolito began.

Giolito started for the White Sox on opening day. Little since has gone to script. He brought a 4.92 ERA to the ballpark Thursday. He departed with one nearing six.

Houston inflicted the worst beating of Giolito's ghastly season. He procured nine outs and permitted seven runs. The Astros struck eight hits against him. Half of them fell for extra bases. Trey Mancini's second-inning solo home run started an avalanche no one on the South Side seemed able to stop.

Giolito somehow limited the damage to Mancini's home run during his first trip through Houston's order. Plate umpire

OPPOSITE: Alex Bregman, who'd given the Astros a 3-0 lead over the White Sox with a two-run double in the third inning, celebrates his two-run homer in the fourth, which made it 10-0.
KAMIL KRZACZYNSKI/USA TODAY SPORTS

RIGHT: Jose Altuve collected two of the Astros' team-record 25 hits, including this one-out single that ignited a three-run third inning at Guaranteed Rate Field.
KAMIL KRZACZYNSKI/USA TODAY SPORTS

Ramon De Jesus assisted Giolito in the first. After Alvarez worked a walk, Bregman watched a full-count fastball sail two inches below the strike zone. De Jesus deemed it a strike.

Bregman protested the poor call. Houston's entire dugout barked at the umpire. Hitting coach Alex Cintrón got ejected for his objections.

"I can't tell you what I was saying," manager Dusty Baker said. "My mother wouldn't like it."

Bregman takes pride in his plate discipline. Few in the sport are better at swinging at strikes and watching balls. This suspect strikeout gave Bregman 60 this season. He has worked 64 walks.

Bregman calmed himself and kept his composure despite the blown call. Three frames later came a chance to forget it. Giolito left a 1-1 four-seam fastball over the heart of home plate. Bregman bludgeoned it into the left-center gap. Altuve and Yuli Gurriel scored as Bregman strolled to second base. Tucker loomed.

Giolito got ahead of Tucker 0-1 before Chicago curiously convened a mound visit.

LEFT: Alex Bregman watches his sixth-inning homer off White Sox pitcher Vince Velasquez take flight. A ninth-inning double would give the third baseman the sixth four-hit game of his career.
KAMIL KRZACZYNSKI/USA TODAY SPORTS

Two days earlier, in an almost identical scenario, the White Sox intentionally balked Bregman off second base in fear he could pick up a pitch grip or catcher's location. The Texas Rangers did it during a series last week, too.

The meeting ended, and Giolitio went to his windup. Bregman broke for third the moment he did. No one covered the bag. Catcher Seby Zavala did not make a throw. The White Sox seemed comfortable with Bregman being anywhere but second base. Bregman seemed comfortable causing problems with their psyche.

Tucker mashed a middle-middle fastball for a single. Bregman scooted home from the base he stole, starting a carousel Chicago could not escape.

"It was fun. It was cool that we could do that to the White Sox," McCormick said. "We were all comfortable today. You could tell, just us going up to the plate, everyone was getting their hits, walks. When we score runs, we do it quick. But that's kind of our offense. It's a good time when everyone is hitting and it's like a merry-go-round."

HOUSTON
ASTROS

Awe-inspiring

Yordan Alvarez hits three titanic home runs as a playoff berth is secured

BY CHANDLER ROME · SEPT. 16, 2022

The day Yordan Alvarez awed the Astros began with no pregame batting practice. He "didn't take a lot" of swings in the team's underground batting cage, either, before authoring the signature moment of his magical season.

"I think that's the most incredible thing I've ever been a part of," utilityman Mauricio Dubón said. "He's the best hitter for a reason. It was so amazing watching him do that and watching what he's been doing all year. He's the best hitter I've ever played with."

Around the Astros clubhouse, the refrain remains the same. Jose Altuve declared it the day Alvarez signed his six-year, $115 million contract extension. On the night Alvarez reached more rarefied air, Justin Verlander joined the chorus.

"He's one of the best hitters I ever played with," Verlander said after firing five hitless innings in a 5-0 win over the A's. "I would say that was a surprising night, but it wasn't."

Alvarez saw nine pitches, took four swings and hit three home runs in his first three at-bats against Oakland starter Adrián Martinez. No Astro had ever struck three home runs against the same pitcher in the same game. Only 11 men in franchise history have ever hit three in one game.

Each of Alvarez's three home runs traveled at least 431 feet. All flew to straightaway center field. According to ESPN Stats and Info, he is the first player to hit three home runs of at least 430 feet since Nelson Cruz on July 25, 2019. Alvarez's three totaled 1,329 feet. He struck each one at least 108.7 mph off the bat.

"That was the best game I've ever seen live from a hitter in my career," catcher Martín Maldonado said.

Hitters have one hangup with Minute Maid Park, an offensive haven with one of baseball's most inviting short porches protruding out in left field. Righthanded pull hitters can lift lazy fly balls for home runs into the Crawford Boxes. Lefties have the luxury of a right-field wall 326 feet away. Neither can conquer center.

Few are more aware than Alvarez. Four months ago, in the bottom of the ninth in a tie game, he hammered a 106.4 mph missile into the left-center gap off Tigers closer Gregory Soto. The baseball traveled 397 feet. Alvarez assumed he hit a walk-off home run and did not run out of the batter's box. The ball died at the warning track, leaving an embarrassed Alvarez to settle for a long single.

The Astros won the game, and Alvarez apologized to his teammates, vowing never again to assume and to always hustle. So in the first inning Friday, he sprinted out of the box after mashing Martinez's middle-middle sinker 434 feet to the same area of the ballpark.

The baseball landed atop the Budweiser bar between the batter's eye and Houston's bullpen, making Alvarez's hustle a moot point. The blast offered more hope for an awakening after Alvarez's abysmal August. He slugged .312 and struck four extra-base hits in 92 plate appearances. Hand problems plagued him. So did poor posture in his batting stance. He posted a 50 percent ground ball rate — more than 12 points above his career average.

"When he's standing too tall at the plate, he crashes with his upper body, and he has no space," hitting coach Alex Cintrón said. "He is jumpy and started hitting ground balls because he had no space. When his upper body leans a little toward the plate, he can see the ball with a better angle. He has space to come inside the ball. (He has) a short landing instead of a big-time leg kick."

Whether Alvarez developed the bad habits because of his bothersome hand — or hands — is another matter entirely. Friday did provide an emphatic end to three days of avoidable drama. Manager Dusty Baker's assertion Wednesday that Alvarez's hands hurt irked the player, who sought out reporters and contradicted his skipper. Alvarez termed it a "miscommunication."

"My body feels great. I think it's felt great all season," Alvarez said Friday. "Obviously, we all know I was battling with a little bit of hand soreness in August. That's not to justify the results there, but that was something that

OPPOSITE: Yordan Alvarez jumps on a first-inning sinker for the first of his three home runs off A's pitcher Adrián Martinez in a 5-0 Astros victory. All told, the dingers traveled 1,329 feet for the Cuban slugger, who in June signed a six-year, $115 million contract extension keeping him in Houston through the 2028 season.
KAREN WARREN/HOUSTON CHRONICLE

RIGHT: With a chance to tie the major league record of four home runs in a game, Yordan Alvarez had the Minute Maid Park faithful on their feet in the seventh inning. Alvarez settled for a single to right field, capping a 4-for-4 night amid a sensational season that saw him slash .306/.406/.613 with 37 homers and 97 RBIs in 135 games. His 1.019 OPS ranked second in the majors to Aaron Judge's 1.111.
KAREN WARREN/HOUSTON CHRONICLE

was affecting me then. After a couple days off the team gave me, I feel better and am just continuing on."

Perhaps Friday offered validation for Baker. However clumsily the reasoning was conveyed, Wednesday's off day did work wonders. Alvarez has had six hits since. Four have fallen for extra bases. He crushed a flat changeup from Martinez for another home run Friday, giving him two in three innings.

"He was in a little funk there, but watching him get ready at the right time is scary," Dubón said.

Half-filled champagne flutes sat strewn on a table a few feet away from Dubón's locker. The team commemorated its sixth consecutive postseason appearance with a small toast and some brief speeches. Baker addressed the group, as did a few players.

Reaching the playoffs has become routine for a franchise with five straight American League Championship Series appearances. Acknowledging the moment is mandatory, but Houston has far loftier goals. For the team to reach them, this version of Alvarez must re-emerge.

The Astros saw flashes of it last October when Alvarez captured ALCS MVP honors. He threatened Aaron Judge in the home run race during the first half of the season before fading thus far in the second. Recency bias can dominate some baseball discourse. Few in the Astros' clubhouse forgot the recent past.

"The whole year has been unreal," Dubón said. "It's unreal, but at the same time, we're not surprised. It's normal, but at the same time, that's how good he is. When he hit the third home run ..."

Dubón stopped mid-sentence and stared. He could not find adequate words. Few of his teammates could, either. Alvarez did something to a baseball only a select few in this sport can claim. He arrived at home plate after Jeremy Peña struck Martinez's hanging

LEFT: Yordan Alvarez, left, and Jeremy Peña went back-to-back in the dugout and at the plate in the fifth inning. After the rookie shortstop launched a home run onto the train tracks beyond left field at Minute Maid Park, Alvarez joined Jeff Bagwell (three times) and Glenn Davis (twice) as the only Astros with multiple three-homer games. Alvarez's first such game was in 2019 at Baltimore.
KAREN WARREN/HOUSTON CHRONICLE

ider onto the train tracks beyond left field.

Though he had a lefthanded reliever arming, A's manager Mark Kotsay allowed Iartinez to face Alvarez a third time. The ookie fired a first-pitch sinker. It grooved to the middle of Alvarez's strike zone. lvarez directed it toward his bullpen.

"I've never seen a ball fly that far," said Phil Iaton, who was warming up when Alvarez it the ball. "I was initially thinking it might nd in the bullpen, but it cleared the bull-en and up on that party deck. I don't think ey've ever had a baseball up there before."

The home run traveled 464 feet. According to Baseball Savant, only one of Alvarez's 97 career home runs is longer — the 469-foot missile he struck against A's starter Paul Blackburn on May 30.

"It's pretty cool when a major league player can make other major league players be in awe," Verlander said. "It's not something that happens all too often. That was kind of one of those moments where everyone was like, 'My goodness.' It's just incredible what he's able to do. I've only seen a few guys be able to do stuff like that over the course of my career."

Asked after the game whether he could hit a ball farther, Alvarez cracked a smile and presumed he could.

"I didn't know it was possible to hit that there," Trey Mancini said. "Sometimes balls seem to die a little bit in center field here. That trampolined off his bat and went to a place I didn't know guys could hit it here. If anyone can do it, it's him."

Added Alex Bregman, who watched it all unfold from the on-deck circle: "I was walking up to the plate, and I was still in shock of how far that ball went. For it to be the third one, that's insane. But that's what he's capable of doing. He's unbelievable."

POSTSEASON
THE WEST
IS OURS

Never gets old

\stros clinch fifth American League West championship in six years

Y DANIELLE LERNER · SEPT. 19, 2022

ST. PETERSBURG, Fla. — Dusty Baker was on the lookout. His eyes, nshielded by the customary ski goggles, arted back and forth, scanning for danger s corks popped and droplets drenched the rp-covered visitors' clubhouse at Tropicana ield. The Astros manager stopped talking id-sentence when he spotted Yordan lvarez lurking with a golden bottle in hand.

"Hey, Grande, no!" Baker cautioned his ugger. The manager gestured to his uncov-red eyes and said in Spanish, "No lentes," r, "No glasses."

It was with clear eyes that many inside nd outside the Astros organization saw e club's potential to repeat as American eague West champions, but what appeared n inevitable conclusion to many arrived still n surprisingly dominant fashion.

Monday's 4-0 win over the Rays allowed e Astros to wrap up their fifth division title n six years, a remarkable feat of consistency at Baker was in the midst of describing hen he was finally doused with champagne nd beer by Alvarez, Aledmys Díaz and ance McCullers Jr.

"We didn't know what we had in spring aining," said Baker, who has won nine di-sion titles in his 25-year managerial career, e last two with Houston. "We expected to in it, but we didn't know we were gonna in it by this much. But they just grinded nd grinded and grinded. That's the key. They were consistent every month, and these guys love each other. That's what I love."

The Astros' division-clinching win kept them 15 games ahead of the second-place Mariners at the top of the AL West standings, a gulf so wide no challenger has gotten closer than 10 games back since mid-July.

"Just the players in this locker room putting it all together," Astros general manager James Click said when asked for the key to the team's success. "We had high hopes for this roster, but you never know — 162 games can do weird things to teams, and the best-laid plans can get blown up by the end of April. The players in this locker room know what they need to do in order to win, and they went out, and they did it."

They did it despite losing, over the last several years, a contingent of All-Star players who constituted an embarrassment of riches. The departures of Gerrit Cole, George Springer and Carlos Correa after each of the last three seasons did not deter the Astros from yet another division title and their sixth consecutive postseason berth.

"We let go some good players, but we brought some good players, too," said second baseman Jose Altuve, whose leadoff home run set the Astros on their way in the clincher. "We're really happy here. Obviously, George, Cole and Carlos are really good players, but like I said, we've got to keep playing, and we're happy with the guys we have here."

Altuve, the longest tenured member of the current Astros, is by now an expert at staying mostly dry during boozy celebrations. He remained out of the fray Monday, content to soak it all in without literally getting soaked.

The same could not be said for newly minted MLB record-holder Framber Valdez, who a day after pitching his 25th consecutive quality start danced gleefully underneath showers of bubbly with a green bag protecting his meticulously woven locks.

When the champagne began to run out, pitchers Cristian Javier and Héctor Neris scooped ice cubes out of the coolers and threw them into the air like glistening confetti.

Neris signed a two-year deal with the Astros last winter after spending eight seasons with the Phillies. The veteran reliever secured the final three outs against the Rays and was at the center of almost every celebratory champagne spraying in the postgame clubhouse.

"I'm so happy today," Neris said. "Thank you, Houston, for supporting me here, and I'll be here for a long time. Championship! ... I came for that, and I feel right now that the decision I made is the right decision."

Alvarez, a power hitter whose looming presence in the batter's box cannot be ignored, stealthily poured champagne down the spine of anyone foolish enough to turn his back. His victims included Baker and, on two separate occasions, ace Justin Verlander

OPPOSITE: Justin Verlander plays frontman for a champagne jam after the Astros secured their fifth American League West title in six years with a 4-0 victory over the Tampa Bay Rays at Tropicana Field. To the immediate left behind Verlander is lefthanded reliever Will Smith, who had closed out the Atlanta Braves' 2021 World Series triumph over Houston and was acquired for pitcher Jake Odorizzi the night before the Aug. 2 trade deadline.
KAREN WARREN/HOUSTON CHRONICLE

RIGHT: Hunter Brown, rated the top prospect in the Astros organization in 2022, threw three scoreless innings of relief in the AL West clincher over the Rays. After being recalled from the Class AAA Sugar Land Space Cowboys, Brown won his major debut with six shutout innings against the Rangers on Sept. 2 at Minute Maid Park, then picked up another victory in his next start at Detroit, where he grew up admiring future teammate Justin Verlander. From that point, the Astros shifted Brown to the bullpen to prepare for the postseason role he assumed. Over seven total regular-season appearances, the righthander posted a 0.89 ERA and 22 strikeouts in 20 1/3 innings.
KAREN WARREN/HOUSTON CHRONICLE

- who managed to keep a straight face hen Alvarez drenched him as he spoke to porters.

The 39-year-old Verlander's vigorous ›meback from Tommy John surgery has :en one of the season's best story lines, and ıe results he's achieved are only the tip of ıe iceberg for an Astros starting rotation ıat ended Monday leading the American eague in ERA, WHIP and opponent ıtting average.

"It's really special to be here and experience ıis again," Verlander said. "It could have :en taken away from me with my surgery. ıe personal stuff aside, to be able to experi- ıce this with your teammates is something don't take for granted. I've been a part of a t of teams that have made the playoffs. I've :en here a lot, but you know, I'll never forget ıe of our first years making the playoffs with ıe Tigers. Sean Casey had come over, who ıd 10 years in the league and never made ıe playoffs, and that perspective that those ıys bring, saying how special it is, don't take for granted, that's something that always uck with me."

Verlander, Altuve, Gurriel, McCullers ıd third baseman Alex Bregman are the last remaining members of the Astros' 2017 squad and thus the only players who have been present for all five of the recent division titles. They are well aware of the rarefied air they breathe in Houston.

"It never gets old, but there are guys who have played in the game for a long time who have never been," said Bregman, who drove in the Astros' last two runs with a double. "Then you have guys who made their debut a few weeks ago. So it never gets old. It's always fun. This is why we play the game. We play the game to win."

Trey Mancini was dealt from the Orioles to the Astros at the July trade deadline after experiencing five consecutive playoff-deficient seasons in Baltimore. Prior to Monday, his lone champagne celebration came during his rookie season in 2016, when the Orioles snuck into the AL wild card game on the last day of the regular season.

"At the time, I remember thinking that it was going to be commonplace and that's what happens every year, but that's not the case," Mancini said. "I have been kind of waiting for this moment for a long time. … I remember a couple of teams that clinched against us and thinking that it'd be really cool to be on the other side. So it's nice to be there."

Jeremy Peña, who was on the Astros' taxi squad but did not actually play when the team clinched the division in 2021, celebrated this year as the franchise's starting shortstop and a cornerstone of its future.

Hunter Brown, who contributed three scoreless frames in relief to Monday's victory, emptied a can of beer onto fellow rookie David Hensley's head. One month ago, both were still in Triple-A.

"It's awesome," Brown said. "These guys have worked hard all season, and I just joined recently, but I'm just really happy to be here and be a part of it. I wouldn't rather be any other place."

The finishing touches on Houston's season are still to come, including securing the top playoff seed in the American League and contending with the rigors of an actual post-season run. But Monday was a still-satisfying culmination of what Baker described as a "total team effort."

"Everybody worked as music together," Baker said. "This is what it takes, especially in modern baseball."

ABOVE FAR LEFT: Awesome, baby! With the Astros at the threshold of a division title, manager Dusty Baker enjoys a pregame chat with renowned college basketball analyst Dick Vitale, who became a Rays season-ticket holder at the club's inception in 1998. **KAREN WARREN/HOUSTON CHRONICLE**

ABOVE LEFT: Amid the postgame revelry, Yordan Alvarez douses Baker with bubbly, to the amusement of Astros pitching coach Josh Miller, right. **KAREN WARREN/HOUSTON CHRONICLE**

HOUSTON
30

Century city

n hometown of Tampa, Kyle Tucker becomes Astros' 18th member of 100-RBI club

BY DANIELLE LERNER · SEPT. 20, 2022

ST. PETERSBURG, Fla. — Astros right fielder Kyle Tucker achieved his first career 00-RBI season in his hometown of Tampa on 'uesday, adding a significant milestone to an lready impressive year.

With a contingent of family and friends heering him on from right field, Tucker rove in Jose Altuve on a soaring double in he opening inning for the game's first run and is 100th RBI. His benchmark hit helped the stros to a 5-0 win over the Rays in the second f three games at Tropicana Field.

"Everyone here pushes each other," Tucker aid when asked about his success. "So if I'm truggling or whatever, guys are helping me ut and trying to make me a better player and rying to do the same for everyone else. So I ust try and put together good ABs and help he team."

That Tucker's milestone occurred against a econd-year pitcher considered one of the best tarters in the majors this season was a bonus.

Shane McClanahan entered Tuesday ranked econd among all American League pitchers in ERA and WHIP, trailing only Justin Verlander. Besides Trey Mancini and Christian Vázquez, who played against the Rays in the AL East with their previous teams, none of the Astros had faced McClanahan prior to Tuesday.

That didn't stop Houston from tagging McClanahan for five runs in four innings. After Tucker's RBI, Jeremy Peña added three in the third inning on his 19th home run of the season.

Altuve drew a walk against McClanahan to lead off the fifth inning and scored on Aledmys Díaz's bases-loaded sacrifice fly off Rays reliever Shawn Armstrong. Houston backup catcher Yainer Diaz notched his first major league hit, a two-out double, during a pinch-hit appearance in the eighth inning.

Astros starter Cristian Javier fanned five of the first 11 batters he faced and did not allow a hit until the fifth inning. He finished five scoreless innings on 90 pitches while yielding one hit and four walks and striking out six as the Astros shut out the Rays for the second day in a row.

After Phil Maton, Ryne Stanke and Will Smith threw an inning apiece, Bryan Abreu loaded the bases with one out in the bottom of the ninth. Houston went to Ryan Pressly, who struck out Ji-Man Choi before Christian Bethancourt lined out to second to complete the six-pitcher three-hitter.

Tucker is the 18th player in Astros history with a 100-RBI season and the club's first full-time outfielder to reach the milestone since Carlos Lee in 2009.

"Oh, I love it," Astros manager Dusty Baker said. "This is something that a lot of people never get to, including me. I was pulling for him. I mean, boy, he knocked fire from that ball, too. So now, just go ahead and get some more."

Other current Astros who have reached the century mark in a season are Alex Bregman (2018, 2019), Yuli Gurriel (2019) and Yordan Alvarez (2021).

The rest of the Astros' 100-RBI club members are Lance Berkman, Jeff Bagwell, Moises Alou, Richard Hidalgo, Derek Bell, Bob Watson, Carl Everett, Jeff Kent, Jim Wynn, Lee May, César Cedeño, Glenn Davis and Morgan Ensberg.

Playing his fifth major league season, Tucker was named to his first All-Star team this year and in the second half of the season has continued to improve his 2022 résumé. The 25-year-old, who is arbitration eligible for the first time this winter, also has a career-high 22 stolen bases and is two home runs from matching his personal best of 30 set last season.

Tucker's RBI count remained at 99 after he went 1-for-4 with no RBIs in Monday's series opener against the Rays, but he didn't have to wait long for his opportunity Tuesday. Altuve and Peña started the game with back-to-back singles against McClanahan before Bregman's fly out moved Altuve to third base.

With Alvarez receiving a rest day, Tucker was batting cleanup for the Astros instead of in his customary spot fifth in the order. He took three consecutive balls from McClanahan, then connected on a 97-mph fastball down in the zone.

"They did a really good job of putting some pressure on Shane early in the game in that first inning," Tucker said. "Josey (Altuve) getting on third with less than two outs was huge. The guys in front of me make it a little easier for me when I'm at the plate to get them in. So I mean, the RBIs are more on them than me."

OPPOSITE: Astros right fielder Kyle Tucker, who plated Jose Altuve with a first-inning double, gives two thumbs up to driving in 100 runs for the first time in his career. The right fielder, who hit 30 homers and stole 25 bases, finished the season with 107 RBIs, good for third in the American League behind the Yankees' Aaron Judge (131) and Guardians' Jose Ramirez (126). JONATHAN DYER/USA TODAY SPORTS

ALTUVE
27

Higher standard

Discontent with recent seasons, Jose Altuve puts together one of his best

BY CHANDLER ROME · SEPT. 28, 2022

One day this spring, Jose Altuve sat at his locker and lamented shortcomings so few watching him even saw. Altuve criticized his approach and bemoaned the absence of a "really, really good season." An All-Star selection in 2021 did not suffice, nor did matching his career high with 31 home runs. He authored the season with a skewed mindset he could not correct while in pursuit of a pennant.

Altuve's expectations are enormous and align with a more modern understanding of offensive prowess. He arrived in the major leagues with limited power and prolific bat-to-ball ability. Strength untapped power, and Altuve became infatuated with exploiting it. He pulled the baseball far too much while trying to mash home runs, sacrificing some of his natural ability to hit. Batting averages once hovering around .340 fell below .300.

"You go to 2019, and I think when I hit 30 or 40 points less, I got to a .900 (OPS). That's what I describe as a good season for me. Obviously, you want to do both — .900 and .300," Altuve said this March.

"I think .900 is the new .300 for batting average. I don't want to say I don't want to hit .300 — I do; I want to hit .400 — but 2019 was my last really, really good season."

Seven games separate Altuve from finishing something more than just a "really, really good season." He is close to satisfying all of his aforementioned objectives with one of the most complete seasons of his stellar career. The eight-time All-Star is posting numbers unlike any since 2017, when he captured American League Most Valuable Player honors.

Altuve struck two more home runs during Tuesday's 10-2 annihilation of the Arizona Diamondbacks. The 3-for-4 evening left him slashing .298/.387/.531 after 510 at-bats. The .918 OPS would be his highest in any season since 2017. So would the .387 on-base percentage.

Altuve's .298 batting average matches his clip from 2019, the same season he struck a career-high 31 home runs. Altuve is three away from matching that, too. He hasn't finished a season with an OPS+ over 150 or a wRC+ (weighted runs created) over 160 since 2017. After Tuesday's game, he had a 159 OPS+ and a 162 wRC+.

"Mentally, he knows what he needs to do right now. He has known for a long time, but he's adjusting," hitting coach Alex Cintrón said. "He's working walks, not (focusing) so much on hitting the ball out. He has 28 homers, but he's not trying to hit homers like he was in the past."

Altuve's comments from March offer a clear blueprint for the season he's close to finishing. A more complete plan and an ability to generate better pull-side contact are propelling Altuve back toward his accepted standard.

Few will ever mistake Altuve for a patient hitter, but his ability to work deeper counts this season has been apparent. He is swinging less frequently than at any point in his career and entered Tuesday's game seeing 3.84 pitches per plate appearance — a career high. His walk rate has spiked to 11 percent after 11 seasons of never eclipsing 9.7 percent.

Do not mistake this for a total change in style. Altuve still ambushes at will. He is 39-for-104 (.375) when putting the first pitch of his plate appearance in play this season.

Twenty-one of the first-pitch hits have fallen for extra bases, including a double against D-Backs starter Zach Davies in the fifth inning Tuesday. Altuve kept his hands inside and laced a sinker down the left-field line, the type of pull-side contact he's continued to produce all season.

Last season, Altuve pulled the baseball at a 49.7 percent clip — the highest mark of his career. This spring, both Altuve and Cintrón acknowledged the second baseman became pull-happy and sold out for home runs into Minute Maid Park's short porch.

Altuve struck both of his home runs Tuesday into that same spot. He's still pulling the ball 46.1 percent of the time, according to Baseball Savant, but the fifth-inning double demonstrated a difference from last season.

"It's a better pull because it's on a line," Cintrón said. "It used to be on the ground. If you look at it last year, it was a lot of

OPPOSITE: The Astros' all-time leader in batting average at .307, Jose Altuve continued his ascension on several career charts for the franchise in 2022. By season's end, he ranked third in doubles (379); fourth in runs (986), hits (1,935), extra-base hits (600) and stolen bases (279); and fifth in home runs (192) and games (1,578).
KAREN WARREN/HOUSTON CHRONICLE

RIGHT: In a 5-2 victory over the Rangers and starting pitcher Taylor Hearn on May 22 at Minute Maid Park, Jose Altuve hit one of his 12 leadoff homers for the 2022 season, tying a club record George Springer set in 2019. The only player in MLB history with more was Alfonso Soriano, who hit 13 for the 2003 Yankees. **JON SHAPLEY/ HOUSTON CHRONICLE**

OPPOSITE: Altuve, a three-time AL batting champion and the league's Most Valuable Player in 2017, ranked fourth in the majors with a .920 OPS in 2022. He slashed .300/.387/.533 with 28 homers, 103 runs, 57 RBIs, and 18 stolen bases in 19 attempts. **KAREN WARREN/HOUSTON CHRONICLE**

ground balls. They started shifting him to the pull side. Now he's able to hit line drives or homers as opposed to the ground balls he used to hit."

Altuve has paired the better pull contact with a clear intent to steal more bases. He's swiped 18 bags this season after totaling 13 in the past three combined, offering a flashback to who he once was.

Altuve might never again approach 30 stolen bases like he did from 2012-17, but he's also a different type of player. He's more dynamic and has added more power. He can alter the game with one swing instead of settling for infield singles. Marrying the two this season has transformed him.

"He's trying to maintain his on-base percentage, OPS, and understands the numbers and what he needs to do to help the team (and) help himself," Cintrón said. "That's the difference between past years and this year."

franklin
HOUSTON
27

HOUSTON
ASTROS
35

As good as ever

n first season after Tommy John surgery, 39-year-old Justin Verlander cements Cy Young case

BY CHANDLER ROME · OCT. 4, 2022

Justin Verlander's coronation came a month early and with his club still in earch of its ultimate prize. More consequen-ial games loom for the Astros' ageless ace, a nan who continues to defy convention while aving his path to Cooperstown. Verlander's nost meaningful innings will arrive across he next few weeks while his team chases second consecutive American League ennant.

Tuesday toasted Verlander's remarkable eturn from elbow reconstruction, even if e seemed in no mood to reflect. Personal ccolades mean little for Verlander until the Astros accomplish their foremost objective. 'erlander treated the start like the 27 preced-ng it, even with an ERA title and Cy Young Award within reach.

"The last few starts, it was like the ecretariat movie," Verlander said. "He's eading by so much, having a great race, and he trainer is like, 'Just don't fall off.' That's ow I felt. I just kept reminding myself, Finish strong. Let's not try to limp home or any particular reason just because I want o finish with whatever flashy numbers there re.' "

Verlander fired five fabulous innings and ulfilled both goals. The season's penultimate ame ended as another exclamation point or one of this generation's greatest pitchers, ne who seems to author history each time he toes the rubber.

Verlander finished his astonishing come-back season with the sort of stifling perfor-mance around which he has built his legacy. He struck out 10 batters across five hitless innings against a reserve-laden Philadelphia Phillies lineup.

Hunter Brown and Héctor Neris brought the Astros within three outs of a no-hitter be-fore Will Smith surrendered a clean single to Garrett Stubbs in the ninth. Smith allowed two more hits but left the bases loaded to preserve a 10-0 win.

Verlander faced 16 batters. Five put the ball in play. He looked like a man who could have completed the no-hitter himself. The nearing postseason made it impossible. A small cut on the top of his right hand, which bled at points during the start, only exacer-bated matters.

Verlander entered the start on a pitch count, both to preserve his arm and afford Houston's relievers some work before an upcoming five-day layoff. As a result, the Astros removed Verlander from a no-hitter for the third time this season inside Minute Maid Park.

"This was a tuneup for the playoffs," manager Dusty Baker said. "We wanted to get him the victory, of course, and wanted him to win the ERA title as well. He was magnificent."

Verlander will enter next season still in search of his fourth no-hitter. Cementing his third American League Cy Young Award sufficed Tuesday.

Since the American League began in 1901, only 57 of its qualified starters have finished a full season with anything lower than a 1.80 ERA. Verlander fired five scoreless innings Tuesday to become the 58th.

His 1.75 clip is the lowest for an American League starter since Pedro Martinez man-aged a 1.74 mark in 2000 en route to his second consecutive AL Cy Young Award and third Cy Young overall. Verlander should notch his third in November, nothing short of remarkable for a man with a brand new right elbow and four months shy of his 40th birthday.

"I think I'm probably the least surprised person that I'm here. Everyone wants to ask mec, 'How amazed are you?' For me, I'm not," Verlander said.

"I know how hard I worked. I know how good I felt. I know how good the rehab went, and I know how good my body felt coming into the season. To me, this was maybe not what was supposed to happen but what I expected to happen. I thought I would be me when I'm healthy, which is usually pretty good."

The entire evening amounted to a glori-fied scrimmage. As he did Monday, Baker

OPPOSITE: Coming off Tommy John surgery for a right elbow injury that sidelined him in July 2020, Justin Verlander looked like his old self in 2022, posting an 18-4 record with an MLB-leading 1.75 ERA and 0.83 WHIP in 175 innings. The ERA bested the previous club record of 1.87 registered by Roger Clemens in 2005. Verlander's victory total was second in the majors to the 21 of the Braves' Kyle Wright. **KAREN WARREN/ HOUSTON CHRONICLE**

RIGHT: Passing John Smoltz, CC Sabathia, Curt Schilling, Bob Gibson, Pedro Martinez, Fergie Jenkins and Max Scherzer along the way, Justin Verlander in 2022 moved from 19th to 12th on the all-time strikeout list with 3,198, topping Scherzer by five among active pitchers. His 18 victories gave Verlander 244 for his career.
KAREN WARREN/HOUSTON CHRONICLE

removed most of his everyday players after three plate appearances apiece. Verlander exited after 77 pitches against a team that seemed like it should be anywhere else.

The Phillies secured their first postseason berth in 11 years Monday night. Champagne celebrations carried well into Tuesday morning. A lineup of substitutes sobered up in time to face Verlander. None of Nick Castellanos, J.T. Realmuto, Rhys Hoskins or Kyle Schwarber played, prompting Baker to josh about the "All-Star lineup on the bench."

Two-time National League Most Valuable Player Bryce Harper led off to afford Verlander some semblance of competition. Harper swung through a full-count slider to start the game and set an unmistakable tone.

Two-hole hitter Alec Bohm bounced out before Verlander engineered another historic run. He struck out the next eight batters he saw, matching a franchise record Don Wilson and Jim Deshaies accomplished.

In his 244th career victory, Verlander also moved from 14th to 12th on the all-time strikeout list with 3,198, passing Fergie Jenkins (3,192) and, at least for now, former Detroit Tigers teammate Max Scherzer (3,193).

"This guy is a horse," Baker said. "He's been great all year, other than when he was out that period of time. It's great to have him on the mound. The team is excited. The fans are excited. I think baseball is excited when he's on the mound on a national stage like that."

Verlander finished six of those eight

LEFT: Exercising caution with Justin Verlander's surgically repaired elbow – and a late-August calf injury that sent him to the injured list for 2 1/2 weeks – the Astros on three occasions removed their 39-year-old ace from a game in which he had allowed no hits, twice after five innings and once after six.
MARK MULLIGAN/HOUSTON CHRONICLE

consecutive punchouts with his slider. He flashed his rarely used changeup in a 1-2 count against Bryson Stott during the second. Stott swung through the pitch while it ran into the other batter's box, the clearest indication of the chasm between hurler and hitters.

A four-pitch walk to Brandon Marsh in the fifth was Verlander's only blemish. He needed 20 pitches to finish the frame and strand him at first. Matt Vierling bounced into a fielder's choice to conclude the only stressful sequence of this simple night.

A crowd of 32,032 came to a crescendo when he did. Verlander shuffled his feet toward a far set of stairs on the first-base dugout. Realization hit before he touched the first step. He doffed his cap toward the fans, who roared in approval at the completion of a comeback.

"I'm obviously very pleased with how it turned out but, obviously, don't have much time to celebrate," Verlander said. "Have to look forward to the postseason, getting my mechanics where they need to be, fine-tuning things and just making sure everything is healthy and good to go.

"I do appreciate it. A lot of hard work went into it. A lot of growth as a person behind the scenes allowed me to appreciate it even more and be in the moment."

60
adidas
enjoy
POSTSEASON

ALDS GAME 1 // ASTROS 8, MARINERS 7

Wondrous wallop

Yordan Alvarez, in stupendous fashion, completes stunning comeback with three-run walk-off homer

BY CHANDLER ROME · OCT. 11, 2022

They will talk on barstools or by water coolers with pure glee, picture-perfect memory and perhaps a hint of hyperbole about the afternoon when Yordan Alvarez added his name to a list of legends propelling the Astros through their golden era. A fan base and franchise conditioned for October success sat through eight innings resembling anything but. The ace delivered a dud, and so did the leadoff man. On two separate occasions, one strike separated Houston from a loss to its little brother in the American League West.

Then, at 6:14 p.m., Mariners manager Scott Servais sauntered to the mound with a confident gait and grand plan. He raised his left hand, summoned the reigning American League Cy Young Award winner, and watched his nightmare unfold. Five consecutive AL Championship Series appearances leave the Astros well-versed in wrecking dreams and spoiling seasons.

In Game 1 of this year's AL Division Series, Alvarez delivered the type of dagger this franchise somehow had still not supplied. His three-run homer against Robbie Ray on Tuesday afternoon handed Houston an improbable 8-7 victory. It was the first walk-off home run in postseason history for a team trailing by multiple runs and the first with two outs since Kirk Gibson's blast off Dennis Eckersley in Game 1 of the 1988 World Series. Among the iconic playoff moments authored during this marvelous Astros era, none matched the majesty of what Alvarez and two rookie teammates teamed to accomplish during a span of 17 minutes in the ninth inning.

With the Astros an out away from a series deficit, Alvarez struck a 93.2 mph sinker so high and with such force that few even saw it land. No one needed to. The 41,125 who gathered here — and the thousands more who will claim they were at Minute Maid Park — accepted the result from the moment barrel met baseball. It left Alvarez's bat at 116.7 mph, harder than any of the 98 home runs he'd hit in his three-year major league career.

Alvarez gazed at the baseball's trajectory before flipping his bat and bounding around the bases. A mob scene formed at home plate while a crowd vacillated from silence to unhinged delirium.

"I was top step, bro," rookie David Hensley said. "I was already waiting for it. I was manifesting it, to be honest. It happened, and I jumped out. I think I may have been the first one on the field."

Houston spent eight innings inviting Seattle to win. The ninth illustrated the chasm between these two clubs. Experience is a team's best trait in October. None of the four surviving American League participants has more than the Astros.

Still, they played as poorly as one could fathom for most of this Tuesday matinee. Ace Justin Verlander surrendered 10 hits and six earned runs across four forgettable frames. He made 29 postseason starts preceding this one. Only once had he allowed six earned runs.

Seattle held two separate four-run leads and, for eight innings, limited the Astros to one hit with a runner in scoring position. Alex Bregman breathed life into a seemingly hopeless situation with a two-run homer against reliever Andrés Muñoz in the eighth. Yuli Gurriel struck a single to send Trey Mancini up as the tying run. Mancini struck out and stranded his third baserunner of the game.

"We've been down in games before in the postseason, and the mentality always stays the same," Bregman said. "Guys know that it comes down to strictly execution in the postseason."

The feeling spreads across the clubhouse, one breaking in a few fledgling playoff participants. Teammates and coaches stress

OPPOSITE: Yordan Alvarez struck Robbie Ray's 0-1 fastball with such ferocity that he and everyone present at Minute Maid Park knew the left fielder had launched a three-run walk-off homer to beat the Mariners in the ALDS opener. Alvarez, whose third-inning double plated the Astros' first two runs, became only the second player in MLB postseason history to hit a game-ending homer with his team down to its last out. Kirk Gibson, whose two-run blast off Dennis Eckersley pushed the Dodgers past the A's in Game 1 of the 1988 World Series, was the first. KAREN WARREN/HOUSTON CHRONICLE

RIGHT: Yordan Alvarez was unable to corral Ty France's fourth-inning fly to left off Justin Verlander, resulting in a two-out RBI double that gave the Mariners a 6-2 lead. But Alvarez got what proved to be a crucial assist when he gunned down France at the plate on a single by the next batter, Eugenio Suárez.
KAREN WARREN/HOUSTON CHRONICLE

LEFT: The Astros had cut the margin to 7-5 when, in the top of the ninth, right fielder Kyle Tucker robbed Seattle rookie phenom Julio Rodriguez of a third extra-base hit with this catch for the second out. Rodriguez scored three times in the game's first four innings, during which he walked, hit a two-run double, and tripled.
JON SHAPLEY/HOUSTON CHRONICLE

shrinking the moment. Before the game, Alvarez said he spoke to many of the club's young players about what lay ahead.

"We've told them, just like in the regular season, it's the same ballgame," Alvarez said through an interpreter. "The only thing, you're probably going to hear a little bit more noise because of the fans, but just continue to play the same game, stay focused. The goal is the same, which is to win."

At least two batters needed to reach for Alvarez to bat in the ninth. The two who did were rookies playing in their first postseason game. Manager Dusty Baker pinch-hit Hensley for Aledmys Díaz. Hensley had never taken a postseason plate appearance, had appeared in just 16 major league games, and is perhaps the 26th man on Houston's roster.

Now, with one out, he stared toward Paul Sewald, one of the interchangeable righthanders in Seattle's stout bullpen. Sewald brought a team-leading 20 saves and 0.77 WHIP into the appearance. He generated a groundout from Christian Vázquez before falling behind Hensley 2-1.

"I felt prepared to be in there and did what I was supposed to do," Hensley said. "(Nerves) are definitely there, but when you're prepared and feel like you're ready to go, they subside. You hold them down. We prepared. ... Got an idea of what he was going to throw and tried my best to execute to the best of my ability. Stay patient and try to look for a pitch to hit."

Hensley saw seven pitches. He fouled two two-strike fastballs before being grazed by another, allowing hope to flicker and Jose Altuve to arrive as the tying run. Sewald struck him out on four pitches, finishing an 0-for-4 day for a man the club relies so heavily upon.

Up strode shortstop Jeremy Peña, who had to know Sewald's plan. Pitchers pounded Peña with sliders all season. He whiffed

RIGHT: The Astros pulled within two on Alex Bregman's two-run homer in the eighth, putting Fabian Izaguirre, right, and Brenna Williamson in a state of fandemonium. **YI-CHIN LEE/HOUSTON CHRONICLE**

OPPOSITE: Jeremy Peña, right, whose two-out single in the ninth allowed Yordan Alvarez to come to the plate with two runners aboard, gets the drop on the Astros hero, whose walk-off homer was the seventh in the club's postseason history. The others were hit by Alan Ashby (1981 NLDS vs. Dodgers), Jeff Kent (2004 NLCS vs. Cardinals), Chris Burke (2005 to end NLDS vs. Braves), Carlos Correa (2019 ALCS vs. Yankees and 2020 ALCS vs. Rays) and Jose Altuve (2019 to end ALCS vs. Yankees). **KAREN WARREN/HOUSTON CHRONICLE**

against them at a 38.2 percent clip. Sewald snuck one by him to put Peña in an 0-2 count. Houston stood one strike from a loss. Sewald spun two more sliders to try to finish it.

Peña let one skip in the dirt. He stayed back on the next and laced it into shallow center field.

"They have probably dreamt about moments like this," Baker said, "and dreams can come into reality."

With one swing, they did. Peña's single prompted Servais to summon a man Houston has handled. Ray is a threat to every team in baseball aside from the Astros. They scored 13 earned runs during the 10⅔ innings he threw against them this season.

Ray had made two relief appearances since 2014. Servais called him a bullpen "bullet, so to speak, for that type of scenario." Ray is lefthanded, but otherwise, the decision defies logic. The sight of Ray entering the game sent Alvarez to an iPad. He huddled with hitting coach Alex Cintrón. The duo presumed Ray would try to establish the inner half with his sinker — a pitch Ray only started throwing in July.

"I knew that he was going to try to attack me," Alvarez said through an interpreter. "He wasn't going to pitch around me. I just went out there and just tried to make good contact."

On the first pitch, he did. Alvarez fouled it back into the net behind home plate. For some reason, Ray returned with another. The rest, as Baker said, is a dream, an out-of-body experience for a slugger who often makes magnificence seem routine.

"I don't think it's about Robbie Ray," catcher Martín Maldonado said. "I think it's more of having our best hitter in the box. It didn't matter if it was Robbie Ray or Sewald. We didn't give up. We had our best hitter in the box and knew something could happen."

ASTROS
44
HOUSTON

STROS
27
60
adidas

ALDS GAME 2 // ASTROS 4, MARINERS 2

Power ball

With go-ahead two-run homer, Yordan Alvarez yields another huge payoff

BY DANIELLE LERNER · OCT. 13, 2022

The legend he's created in Houston is not yet enough for Yordan Alvarez, who both dwarfs and creates seminal moments when he brings a bat off his left shoulder. The Astros slugger's prodigious power is the stuff of fantasy, or nightmares, depending on who is telling the story.

Two days after devastating Seattle with a three-run walk-off homer, Alvarez served up a go-ahead two-run blast Thursday to propel the Astros to a 4-2 win and a 2-0 lead in the American League Division Series for a sixth straight year.

Alvarez became the fourth player in franchise history to homer in each of the Astros' first two postseason games, a melding of mammoth swings that encompass an otherworldly display.

The 25-year-old is the first player in MLB postseason history to hit multiple career go-ahead home runs in the sixth inning or later. His victims in back-to-back ALDS games at Minute Maid Park this week were a former American League Cy Young winner and a two-time All-Star considered a pitching anomaly. Alvarez is an outlier all of his own, with hitting metrics that jump off the page and a name destined to cause generations of Mariners fans to break into cold sweats.

Novellas devoted to Alvarez's exploits frequently wax poetic about his opposite-field ability, his power and his imposing build. Asked how he would describe himself as a hitter, though, Alvarez chose a different adjective.

"I would say intelligent," Alvarez said through an interpreter after Game 2. "I think whenever I go up to the plate, I try to visualize the different kinds of results that I could get up there when I'm hitting. If everything goes according to plan, we'll get a positive result. Obviously, there's still a pitcher out there who is trying to get me out."

The Astros trailed 2-1 in the bottom of the sixth with two outs and had reached base just three times against Luis Castillo, an intrepid hurler revered for his combination of high velocity and movement. Alvarez's first two at-bats of the game resulted in a weak-contact groundout and a fly out.

Alvarez returned to the plate determined to make contact again. He spoiled one 98 mph sinker foul, then reached outside the strike zone for another and launched a two-run blast into the Crawford Boxes to reclaim Houston's lead — again demonstrating why his at-bats command rapt attention from those bearing witness on a screen, in a stadium seat, or on the top step of the dugout.

"You don't go to the bathroom, you know? I mean, you wait. You hold it until after he hits," Astros manager Dusty Baker said. "You don't talk to anybody. You just pay attention. We've got the same anticipation. I mean, it's hard to keep hitting it out, but when you're concentrating at a high level like that, he's getting a pitch, and he's not missing it."

Just as huge as Alvarez's Game 2 homer was the Astros' pitching that preceded it, executed by a ninth-year veteran reliever making his postseason debut. Héctor Neris departed the only major league team he'd ever known last winter to seek playoff exhilaration in Houston.

Some three weeks after the former Philadelphia Phillie secured the final out at Tampa Bay to clinch the Astros' AL West title, Neris entered against the Mariners in the sixth inning with the bases loaded and two outs. He escaped with a huge out that kept it a one-run game, enabled Alvarez's heroics, and ultimately earned him the win.

Rookie shortstop Jeremy Peña, who batted second for the Astros directly in front of Alvarez, set the table for him for the second day in a row with a two-out single in the bottom of the sixth.

"When you have Yordan behind you, they kind of attack you a little bit more because they don't want to face him," Peña said. "It's impressive what he's doing. I've got the easy part."

Kyle Tucker's second-inning solo home run

OPPOSITE: You want an encore? To the delight of Jose Altuve, left, Yordan Alvarez provided one. After hitting a three-run walk-off homer to end Game 1 against the Mariners, Alvarez gave the Astros a lead they never relinquished in Game 2 with a two-run long ball that put them up 3-2 in the sixth inning. That made Alvarez the fourth Astros player to homer in each of the first two games of a postseason, joining Alex Bregman (2018), Colby Rasmus (2015) and Ken Caminiti (1999). KAREN WARREN/HOUSTON CHRONICLE

RIGHT: Alex Bregman delivers an eighth-inning RBI single to give the Astros a 4-2 lead, thwarting the strategy of Mariners manager Scott Servais, who didn't want to risk another Yordan Alvarez long ball. After Jeremy Peña had walked with two outs, Servais intentionally walked Alvarez, putting Peña in scoring position for Bregman. **KAREN WARREN/HOUSTON CHRONICLE**

gave the Astros an immediate advantage for the first time this series, but they soon fell behind after a predicament created by southpaw Framber Valdez, who started Game 2 of the Division Series for Houston for a third straight year.

Valdez entered Thursday with a 1.94 career ERA in nine games (seven starts) against the Mariners and proceeded to work 5⅔ innings while yielding two runs (one earned), four hits and three walks while striking out six on 92 pitches. He retired 10 of the first 11 batters he faced before a one-out walk issued to Eugenio Suárez conjured a troublesome version of Valdez from 2019.

In a 26-pitch fourth inning, Valdez threw two more balls than strikes, the most frustrating in his mind being ball four to Suárez. Astros catcher Martín Maldonado, the man to whom Valdez credits much of his success, attempted to frame the pitch but did not get the strike call on a cutter clearly outside the zone.

Valdez's displeasure hampered his command and fueled the Mariners. Mitch Haniger's ground ball ricocheted off the protruding corner of the stands in foul territory and rolled into no man's land between Peña and Alvarez in left field, allowing Haniger and Suárez to take second and third base.

Valdez fielded Carlos Santana's comebacker but, rather than attempt to get Seattle's slow designated hitter out at first base, committed

LEFT: Jeremy Peña, who had been aboard on Yordan Alvarez's sixth-inning homer and would score four of the Astros' 13 runs in the ALDS, maneuvers his way around Mariners catcher Cal Raleigh on Alex Bregman's RBI single in the eighth.
KAREN WARREN/HOUSTON CHRONICLE

an error on a wild throw home. The tying run scored; however, Santana was caught in a rundown between first and second. On Valdez's next pitch, Dylan Moore sliced a two-out single into right field, and Haniger scored from third as the go-ahead run.

The Astros starter escaped the inning without further damage, retired the side on 13 pitches in the fifth, and secured two outs in the sixth before another walk hastened trouble. Santana ripped a double to right field, putting runners on the corners. Valdez fell behind in the count 2-0 to Moore, got to a full count and unleashed a curveball. It missed wide, walking the bases loaded and summoning Baker from the dugout. Valdez handed him the baseball and walked off the field stone-faced, but he later high-fived Cristian Javier in the dugout after Neris procured an inning-ending groundout.

"I wouldn't necessarily say I felt comfortable throwing to them, but it was all about the focus," Valdez said through an interpreter. "I was very focused today, and I felt confident in all my pitches — my sinker, my curveball, and my changeup — to throw all those pitches for strikes. I was able to get to the sixth inning and keep the game where it was and give the team a chance to win."

In June, Alvarez inked a six-year, $115 million contract extension with the Astros. Two months later, his parents and brother obtained visas to the United States from

RIGHT: Mariners fans cheering their team's first playoff appearance since 2001 had taken to balancing footwear on their heads for good luck during Seattle's series with the Blue Jays in the wild card round. Against the Astros, they were merely waiting for the other shoe to drop.
YI-CHIN LEE/HOUSTON CHRONICLE

Cuba and for the first time watched Alvarez play at Minute Maid Park.

The combination unlocked for Alvarez another level of assurance on the field, and his family bore witness to his unfathomable feats against the Mariners this week. After his home run Thursday, Alvarez pointed to his family in the stands and mimed swinging an imaginary bat.

"I think it's helped me a lot, especially my family being here," he said. "I think that it does give me a lot of peace of mind having them here. Yeah, definitely, I do think that it's helped my performance."

Two innings after his go-ahead homer, the Astros still clung to a one-run lead when Alvarez came up to bat with Peña on first base via a two-out walk. This time, the Mariners intentionally walked him to get to Alex Bregman. The third baseman laced a single into right field, and Peña, one of the speediest players on Houston's roster, raced home and made a headfirst slide for a valuable insurance run.

For Baker, the intentional walk to Alvarez with first base occupied, moving Peña into scoring position, evoked memories of another storied slugger he managed earlier in his career.

"That was some Barry Bonds-type stuff there," Baker said. "I mean, that's the ultimate respect."

The way he eviscerates baseballs, records and opponents simultaneously, Alvarez has ensured such respect will never be in short supply.

LEFT: Things were looking up after Ryan Pressly struck out Ty France to seal the Astros' Game 2 victory. During a regular season in which he saved a career-high 33 games, Pressly set a franchise record by retiring 32 consecutive batters over the course of 10 outings spanning June 25 to July 28. The previous mark was 27 by reliever Dave Giusti in 1965.
BRETT COOMER/HOUSTON CHRONICLE

3
ALDS
JP3

Epic!

Jeremy Peña's 18th-inning home run sends Astros to sixth consecutive AL Championship Series

BY CHANDLER ROME · OCT. 15, 2022

SEATTLE — Past the sixth hour of a scoreless game, with delirium near and a Division Series in the balance, a rookie finally functioned like one. Jeremy Peña pounded his chest between first base and second. He repeated this twice after reaching third, perhaps an out-of-body experience for a player who prides himself on poise.

Part of Peña's allure is his stoicism. On Saturday, he shed it for 18 seconds in the 18th inning. Peña parked Penn Murfee's full-count, four-seam fastball over the center-field wall to give Houston a 1-0 victory and American League Division Series sweep of the Seattle Mariners, then paraded around the bases like a boy playing his first baseball game.

Before the series, Peña said he dreamed of playing in the postseason as an 8-year-old. Saturday afforded him a rare chance to act like one.

Peña spent six months maintaining a manner more reserved for a 10-year major leaguer than a rookie trying to replace a legend. His makeup made the Astros comfortable calling him up in Carlos Correa's absence.

The incessant comparisons to Correa did not deter him. Nor did a dismal second-half slump. Peña's defense never suffered. Nor did his demeanor. The Astros anticipated a learning curve but expressed confidence Peña could embrace it. The ALDS rewarded their faith, and they are now headed to a sixth consecutive AL Championship Series.

Calling this a coming of age is disingenuous. Peña played above his pay grade all season. These three games against Seattle afforded the nation a chance to see it. Peña played errorless ball at shortstop and either prolonged or produced game-winning situations in all three victories.

A strike away from making the last out in Game 1, Peña struck a slider to shallow center field for a single. Yordan Alvarez followed with a mammoth walk-off home run. Alvarez chased Peña home with another bomb in Game 2, one made possible only after Peña blooped a two-out single against Mariners ace Luis Castillo. Saturday allowed Peña his own stage, and he seized it.

"You never know until you get there, but you could tell by his brightness in his eyes and his alertness on the field that he wasn't scared and he wasn't fazed by this," Astros manager Dusty Baker said.

Peña scored four of Houston's 13 runs in the series. According to Baseball Savant, he supplied a 1.63 win probability added in the ALDS. Only Alvarez had a higher one.

Peña, who was hitless in his first seven at-bats Saturday, finished 4-for-16 during the three-game series against Seattle. Two of his hits went for extra bases. He struck out just four times and worked a walk, demonstrating a consistent approach and quality of at-bat that were not always present this season.

Peña slashed .243/.267/.398 after the All-Star break. He abandoned his leg kick in mid-September, allowing him to get his front foot down quicker. The adjustment allows Peña to recognize pitches earlier and gives him more time to make a swing decision. His improvement against sliders is a direct result of the retooled stance. Peña's Game 1 single arrived against a two-strike slider from Paul Sewald — after he didn't chase one a pitch before.

Peña saw 3.59 pitches per plate appearance during the regular season. Major league average is 3.89. Peña averaged 3.82 pitches during his 17 ALDS plate appearances. Just four of them featured only one or two pitches. One of those ended with a double.

"I feel like I've just matured," Peña said earlier in the series. "I've matured more as a hitter, you know, staying more with the game plan (and) approach. Approach is everything. So that's been the biggest difference."

Few will ever mistake Peña for a patient hitter. Only six qualified major league hitters

OPPOSITE: After going hitless in seven at-bats, Jeremy Peña produces the only run in the Astros' Game 3 clincher, leading off the 18th inning with a solo homer off Penn Murfee, the ninth of 10 pitchers employed by Seattle in its first postseason home game in 21 years.
KAREN WARREN/HOUSTON CHRONICLE

RIGHT: This show of hands was hardly quick in a game more than six hours old, but Astros second baseman Jose Altuve found Jeremy Peña's go-ahead home run worth the wait. **KAREN WARREN/HOUSTON CHRONICLE**

OPPOSITE: How about a hug? Luis Garcia, the eighth pitcher used by the Astros, had earned one after throwing high-leverage scoreless relief over the last five of the game's 18 innings. Supplying it was Christian Vázquez, who'd been catching since the seventh after pinch-hitting for Martín Maldonado. **KAREN WARREN/HOUSTON CHRONICLE**

swung more frequently than he did during the regular season. In October, an ability to work deeper counts, spoil pitches foul and show a semblance of plate discipline is imperative. Doing so this series — one in which leadoff man Jose Altuve finished 0-for-16 — felt more mandatory.

Peña has cemented himself in the two-hole, hitting behind Altuve and in front of Alvarez. The position almost guarantees Peña a steady diet of fastballs. He slugged .560 and hit .293 against them during the regular season. Murfee threw him five in a row Saturday.

The final one floated in at 88.1 mph. Peña pulverized it to left-center field. He sprinted out of the batter's box, unaware of how the baseball would carry in the Seattle night.

"I was just trying to stay inside the baseball," said Peña, whose hit was the Astros' 11th in the game. "Thought I drove it in the gap."

Center fielder Julio Rodríguez gave chase as if he did. Rodríguez is the presumptive American League Rookie of the Year and one of Peña's close friends. The two took divergent paths to this point. Rodríguez carried his Seattle club to prominence. Houston did not need such heroics from Peña, just the same stoic version of himself the franchise had seen since his arrival.

Rodríguez ran out of room as he reached the warning track. The baseball disappeared over the fence. Peña's unflappable facade faded — and for good reason.

the show.
Mobile
44

POSTSEASON
HOUSTON
60

Mighty pen

After six scoreless innings from Lance McCullers Jr., seven Astros relievers throw a dozen more

Y DANIELLE LERNER · OCT. 15, 2022

SEATTLE — On a baseball field blanketed by a hazy fog, with Seattle's ayoff drought-ending underdog squad at sk of elimination and Houston's juggernaut anchise on the brink of a sixth consecutive merican League Championship Series erth, a marathon pitching duel commenced.

Shadows overtook T-Mobile Park, and the game neared its end, darkness crept . Eight Astros arms had discharged 253 tches over the course of six-plus hours.

Jeremy Peña then lifted up his pitching aff, untying a scoreless game with a solo ome run in the 18th inning. Nine more tches from Luis Garcia in the bottom of e frame completed the Astros' sweep of the Iariners in the AL Division Series.

Houston's 1-0 win in Saturday's 18-inning ame 3 tied the franchise and MLB record r longest playoff game, by innings, in hisry. Three previous postseason games went 3 innings, including Game 4 of the 2005 ational League Division Series, which the stros won 7-6 over the Braves on Chris urke's walk-off homer.

Until Peña's history-echoing blast, the ame hung in the balance as precariously as shoe balanced atop a superstitious Seattle n's head.

The shortstop's heroics accentuated an stros pitching clinic bookended by Lance IcCullers Jr.'s masterful six-inning start and Luis Garcia's five-inning finale.

"This at-bat was not going to be possible if our pitching staff didn't keep us in the ballgame," Peña said. "They dominated all game. Their pitching staff dominated all game. Yeah, these guys have done it all year. So shout-out to them."

The Astros' bullpen finished the 2022 regular season with the lowest ERA (2.80) in the major leagues. It has allowed one earned run in 26 1/3 innings this postseason, including a streak of 18 scoreless since Cristian Javier gave up a solo home run in the seventh inning of Game 1 against the Mariners.

Seven Houston relievers teamed Saturday to cover 12 innings. As the game wore on, the men in the confined space behind left field chugged coffee and Red Bull. Some changed into long sleeves as the air cooled.

"We ran out of water," Astros bullpen catcher Javier Bracamonte said. "We ran out of coffee. We ran out of sunflower seeds. We ran out of a lot of stuff."

"I was watching the time, six hours in the bullpen, and I was like, 'Damn,' " said José Urquidy. "When Peña hit (the homer), it was crazy."

"Inning by inning by inning, it's difficult, because by one pitch, you can lose," Garcia said. "So I was trying to give my best, and I'm glad that I did."

Astros hitters struck out 20 times, a club postseason record. But Astros hurlers matched the Mariners pitch for pitch – Seattle fanned 22 times – and outlasted them in a stalemate the length of two typical games.

The MLB rule that put a runner on second base to start extra innings disappeared with this postseason, a change that foretold the risk of teams burning through pitchers in bonus baseball. The Guardians and Rays played 15 innings in the second game of their AL wild card series, which also ended 1-0 (in Cleveland's favor).

The Astros constructed their ALDS roster with this in mind. They left off lefthanded reliever Will Smith, who closed out last year's World Series against them for the Braves, in favor of carrying all seven of the pitchers who started games for them this season. Three were in the bullpen Saturday: Garcia, Urquidy and rookie Hunter Brown.

Heading into the 12th inning, the trio of starters were the only pitchers left in the Astros' bullpen.

Bracamonte was in the pen for the 18-inning 2005 game against the Braves, when the Astros summoned seven-time Cy Young Award Roger Clemens from the clubhouse to pitch the last three innings in a break-glass-in-case-of-emergency situation.

On Saturday in Seattle, when Garcia returned to the mound for his fifth inning of work following Peña's blast, the Astros still

OPPOSITE: Astros pitcher Lance McCullers Jr. was hyped after striking out Mariners rookie Julio Rodriguez for the third consecutive time to end the fifth inning of ALDS Game 3. Making his first postseason start since leaving Game 4 of the 2021 ALDS against the White Sox with forearm tightness that shelved him for four-plus months in 2022, McCullers allowed a pair of singles and two walks in his six-inning scoreless stint. **KAREN WARREN/HOUSTON CHRONICLE**

RIGHT: The first man out of the Astros bullpen in Game 3, Héctor Neris threw a clean seventh inning with two strikeouts. In 65 1/3 regular-season innings, Neris put up a 1.01 WHIP with 79 K's to 17 walks. It was his initial campaign in Houston after eight years in Philadelphia with no playoff trips. Ironically, his former team would make it to the World Series against his new team. **KAREN WARREN/HOUSTON CHRONICLE**

had Urquidy as the last man in the bullpen. He did not have to leave it.

The scenario was not quite equivalent, but in Bracamonte's estimation, "Luis Garcia was Roger Clemens."

A different future Hall of Famer heaped praise upon Garcia in a champagne-soaked clubhouse.

"Luis, what he did at the end was one of the best pitching performances I've seen in the playoffs," Justin Verlander said. "It was just incredible. I know there was a lot of other guys that were part of it, but just a great all-around effort. Incredible."

Following a 14th-inning stretch during which a Beastie Boys protest anthem blasted from the ballpark sound system, Garcia entered for his first postseason relief appearance. The 25-year-old threw 64 pitches, allowed two hits and fanned six batters. He took the most pride in twice retiring Mariners rookie phenom Julio Rodríguez, including on a line drive for the game's final out.

"I wanted to pitch so bad. I had the opportunity, and I just tried to help th team," Garcia said. "I'm really happy to b part of this right now, and I'm just going keep going."

Before Garcia took over, Brown pitche two innings and retired five of the seven bat ters he faced, including Adam Frazier, wh hit into a 3-6-3 double play. The lone excep tions were on a hard-hit single surrendere to Carlos Santana and a walk to Rodrígue After getting on first base, Rodríguez sto second, but Brown stranded him with a

ning-ending groundout.

"That was one of the coolest baseball games ve ever been a part of," crowed Brown, who id he was 7 in 2005 and unaware of the stros' previous 18-inning playoff game. These guys told me just to execute pitches. hat's first and foremost. That's number one. tick to the plan, try and execute pitches as est you can, and just keep the train rolling."

McCullers began the game on the mound r Houston by dealing six shutout innings, lowing two hits and two walks with seven strikeouts. It marked the second-longest scoreless playoff appearance of his career, topped only by when he shut out the White Sox for 6 2/3 innings in Game 1 of last year's ALDS.

McCullers, who missed the bulk of the season with a forearm issue, threw at least 90 pitches in each of his last seven regular-season starts following his Aug. 13 season debut versus Oakland (81 pitches, six innings). He completed six scoreless frames in Seattle at 88 pitches before Astros manager Dusty Baker brought in Héctor Neris to face a lefty-heavy section of the Mariners' lineup in the seventh.

Neris' 1-2-3 inning kicked off a relief effort that saw Houston allow eight Seattle baserunners through the game's final dozen innings.

"I pitched in the game of my life today," Neris said afterward, his voice hoarse from celebration. "Trust myself, trust everybody here. Because being together is the key for this team."

Rafael Montero, acquired by the Astros

ABOVE LEFT: Against the Seattle team that traded him to Houston in 2021, Rafael Montero contributed a scoreless eighth to the Astros' 18-inning gem. He had a 2.37 ERA and 1.02 WHIP in 2022 and totaled 14 saves in 16 chances. **KAREN WARREN/ HOUSTON CHRONICLE**

ABOVE RIGHT: Bryan Abreu, who emerged as a force in 2022 with a 19-appearance scoreless streak and finished with a 1.94 ERA, fanned two Mariners in a perfect 10th. **KAREN WARREN/HOUSTON CHRONICLE**

ABOVE LEFT: In 2022, Ryne Stanek set an Astros record for qualified relievers, posting a 1.15 ERA that shattered Will Harris' 2019 mark of 1.50. Stanek's 1-2-3 inning in the 11th kept Seattle off the board. **KAREN WARREN/HOUSTON CHRONICLE**

ABOVE RIGHT: Hunter Brown chipped in two scoreless innings, inducing a double play to end the 12th and stranding Julio Rodriguez, who'd stolen second, in the 13th. **KAREN WARREN/HOUSTON CHRONICLE**

OPPOSITE: "Long-suffering Mariners fans" took on new meaning as the scoreboard at T-Mobile Park reflected the zero gravity of their situation. **KAREN WARREN/HOUSTON CHRONICLE**

from Seattle at last year's trade deadline, continued to dismantle his former team. The lean righthander was shut down with an injury after pitching just four games for the Astros last season. This year, Montero held the Mariners to a .118 batting average in six scoreless regular-season innings against them and in this year's ALDS appeared in all three games without allowing a run in 3 1/3 innings.

"I think the hard work has really been the key all season," said Montero, who disputed the notion he is a different pitcher than when he was with Seattle. "Unfortunately last year, I didn't have a good season. But thankfully, we're here celebrating."

Montero's changeup has played especially well against lefthanded hitters this season, and it did again Saturday to produce consecutive eighth-inning outs against Jarred Kelenic and J.P. Crawford. Rodríguez attacked Montero's slider for a two-out double, but Montero escaped with a three-pitch strikeout of Ty France.

Ryan Pressly allowed Seattle to put the winning run in scoring position with one out in the ninth before he procured consecutive outs. In the next two innings, Bryan Abreu and Ryne Stanek, the latter of whom hadn't pitched in 10 days, each retired the side in order.

"These are the games in the playoffs that you live for," Stanek said. "It was just a he of a game. It really was. From start to finis the offense grinded out at-bats. Obviousl things didn't go as smoothly today on th offensive end of the game, but we didn't eas up, and you have to do that in a marathon.

Then came Brown, followed by Garcia.

"Five basically do-or-die innings, and t get the win — that is the most impressiv thing I've seen in a long time, maybe in m career," said Stanek, a sixth-year veteran.

It was indeed do or die for the Astros, an to survive they did the one thing they've dor consistently all season. They pitched.

11 12 13 14 15 16 7 8
Houston 0 0 0 0 0 0 0
Seattle 0 0 0 0 0 0 0
MARINERS
MARINERS
44

ASTROS
35

ALCS GAME 1 // ASTROS 4, YANKEES 2

Strike force

ʼuli Gurriel, Chas McCormick, Jeremy Peña go deep o back 17 K's from Justin Verlander, bullpen

Y BRIAN T. SMITH · OCT. 19, 2022

Justin Verlander was a true ace on a night when one of the best pitchers of this illennium wasn't perfect.

Yuli Gurriel was everything the Astros eeded.

Chas McCormick was everything Minute Iaid Park needed.

Jeremy Peña blasted another October ocket.

And after all the zeros in Seattle — and r four of the initial five innings Wednesday ight — an electric 4-2 victory over the New ork Yankees in Game 1 of this American eague Championship Series felt like an nmediate statement by the AL's best team.

The pennant still runs through Houston.

October, again, belongs to our buzzing owntown ballpark.

And if Dusty Baker's club can do this three ore times, the World Series will soon return Houston.

"I've said this before about our team: here's just zero complacency — ever," erlander said. "We won Game 1, (but) we nderstand that there's a hard road ahead of s still. And we expect everybody to come ut (Thursday) just like we lost this game. hat's the sense of urgency that we always ave, particularly in the playoffs, but that's hy I think these guys are so special. We do that in the regular season as well, but in the playoffs, it's taking it to another level."

There was a theory entering the ALCS that the Yankees might steal the first contest because they were the "hot" team and the Astros had been quietly resting.

That thought was destroyed in the sixth inning as Gurriel and McCormick ignited Minute Maid Park, and you could again power this entire city by running an extension cord into a stadium filled with 41,487 orange-and-blue believers.

"We just keep grinding, keep grinding, and tonight we made more contact than they made," Baker said. "Our bullpen did an outstanding job. That was big of (Ryan) Pressly, because I think that's the first time all year we've summoned him for a four-out save. But he was really good, very good. Then we had some guys have big nights. McCormick had a big night. (Martín Maldonado) got us on the board. Peña had a big night. Yuli hit the ball great."

Harrison Bader made it 1-0 New York after a solo homer to left-center field, and it took Verlander 45 pitches to make it through two frames.

But the presumptive 2022 AL Cy Young winner fought back like a future Hall of Famer. The Astros then hammered the Yankees' pen for three runs after Verlander departed and improved to 6-2 overall this season against the AL's second-best team.

At 6:36 p.m., a 106-win team sprinted onto its field, receiving raucous cheers and throwing the ball around before attempting to knock off New York in the postseason for the fourth time since 2015.

With standing-room-only sections packed and fans decorating the top row at the back of the ballpark, a familiar buzz connected the early innings.

Verlander, who gave up six runs in four innings in his Game 1 start in the AL Division Series, again faced trouble in the third, with Yankees standing on second and third base with one out. But a swinging strikeout of Josh Donaldson was followed by a 98 mph fastball that froze Matt Carpenter, allowing Verlander to keep this Game 1 tied at 1.

"That was huge, because this guy, he can get out of trouble," Baker said. "The strikeout to Carpenter, he dialed it up; he got it together. He was actually better between 80 and 100 (pitches) than he was prior to that."

Verlander wound up retiring the last 11 batters he faced, nine by strikeout, in his six-inning start. His 11 K's for the game pushed him past Clayton Kershaw for the all-time postseason lead with 219 (to Kershaw's 213).

OPPOSITE: Justin Verlander, among four Astros pitchers who put the K in Yankees in the ALCS opener, finishes his outing with a whiff of Matt Carpenter to end the New York sixth. Verlander retired the last 11 men he faced, nine by strikeout, while allowing a run on three hits. His 11 strikeouts for the game upped his career postseason total to an MLB-record 219, six ahead of Clayton Kershaw. By the end of the World Series, Verlander would have 230. KAREN WARREN/ HOUSTON CHRONICLE

RIGHT: All rose for Astros center fielder Chas McCormick when he scored from first base on Martín Maldonado's two-out second-inning double against Yankees starter Jameson Taillon, knotting the game at 1. McCormick would put Houston up 3-1 with a sixth-inning home run off Clarke Schmidt, who had surrendered a tiebreaking dinger to Yuli Gurriel two batters earlier. **KAREN WARREN/HOUSTON CHRONICLE**

Could the Astros' bats back their proud, gutsy ace?

Heck, yes.

Gurriel lined a solo shot to left field. McCormick lifted a solo homer to right field. Minute Maid Park and the Astros' dugout couldn't stop celebrating, and it was suddenly 3-1 after all the zeros dating to Seattle.

"We have a really good lineup, and it seems like if the big guys aren't going, then the bottom of the lineup can get going," said McCormick, who went 2-for-3 with a walk and two runs. "If the bottom of the lineup isn't going, the big guys can get going. It just kind of talks about how complete this team is."

Peña, who's turning Carlos Correa into a distant memory, drilled another Yankees offering in the seventh, and Game 1 was win in waiting.

The rookie shortstop isn't playing like rookie. Peña went 3-for-4 in Game 1 wit three extra-base hits and has homered i back-to-back games.

"He's stepped in and been an impact playe for them," New York manager Aaron Boon said. "He gets a breaking ball like he go

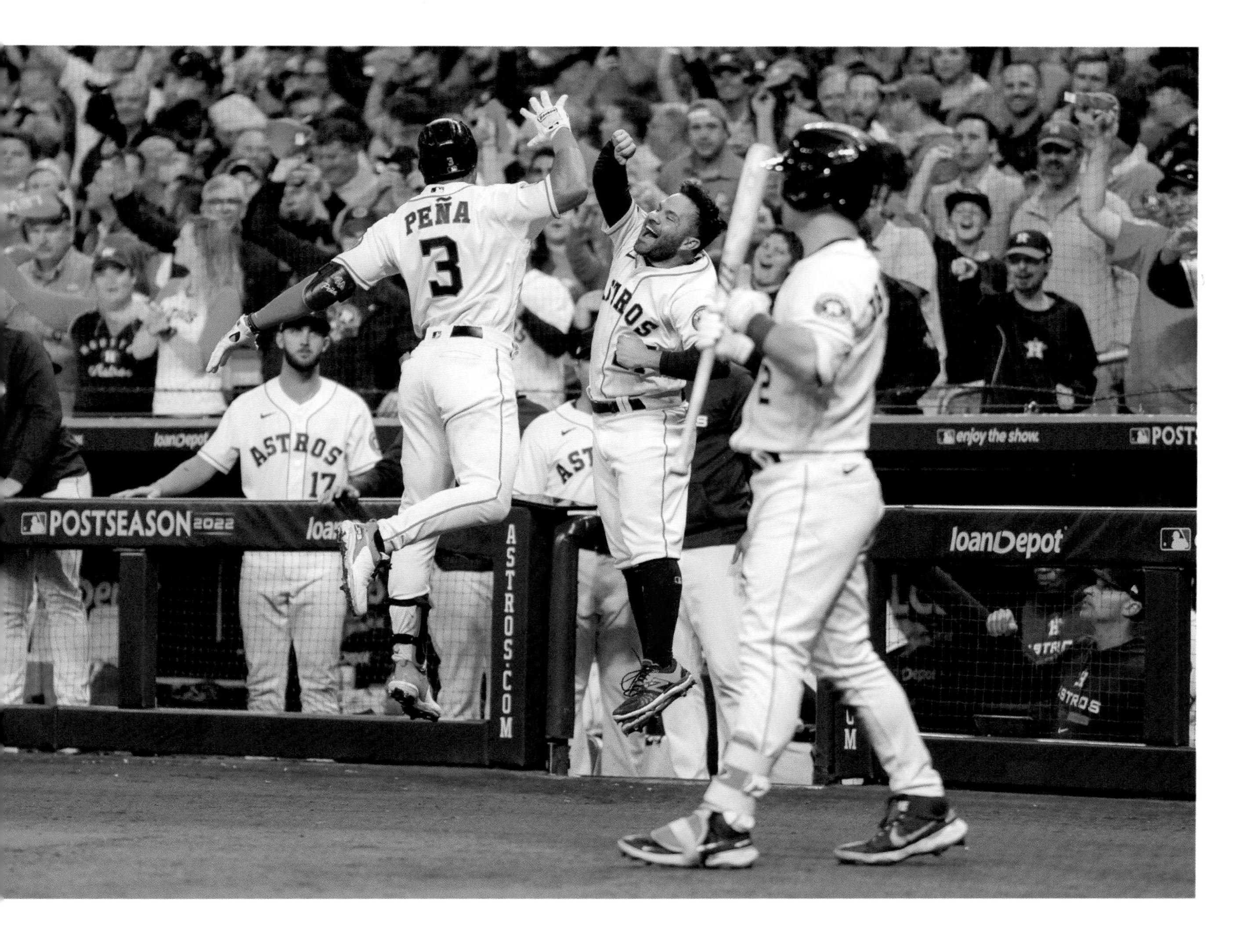

LEFT: After rookie Jeremy Peña rose to the occasion yet again, this time with a seventh-inning homer that put the Astros up 4-1, Jose Altuve elevated his celebration game. **BRETT COOMER/HOUSTON CHRONICLE**

Wednesday), he's done a good job with hose all year. (If) you miss with it, he can o damage with it."

Aaron Judge returned to the plate in the ighth inning. The big name with 62 home uns fanned against Rafael Montero, becoming New York's 14th strikeout victim of the ight, but the Yankees weren't without one ast threat. After Anthony Rizzo homered to make it 4-2, Giancarlo Stanton singled, and Donaldson walked to put the tying runs aboard.

Baker summoned Pressly, who struck out Carpenter – the DH's fourth whiff of the game – and then retired the Yankees in order in the ninth. Pressly's two strikeouts in the final inning gave Astros pitchers 17 for the game. Houston batters struck out only twice, the greatest disparity in postseason history.

Game 1, therefore, went just like the 2015 Wild Card game, 2017 ALCS, '19 ALCS and 2022 regular season.

The Yankees couldn't hang with the Astros because the American League still runs through Houston.

ABOVE: Robert Wilson was among 41,487 fans getting a Minute Maid spark during Game 1 of the American League Championship Series. YI-CHIN LEE/HOUSTON CHRONICLE

RIGHT: With two outs in the New York eighth and fans waving their illuminated cellphones like lighters at a concert, Ryan Pressly warms up to Johnny Cash's "God's Gonna Cut You Down," the signature entrance song of the Astros closer. Pressly struck out Matt Carpenter, then threw a 1-2-3 ninth to notch the first of his three ALCS saves. JON SHAPLEY/HOUSTON CHRONICLE

loanDepot
ALCS
Minute Maid
loanDepot
ALCS
loanDepot
121

enjoy
the show.
POSTSEASON 2022

ALCS GAME 2 // ASTROS 3, YANKEES 2

One big swing

Alex Bregman's three-run homer holds up as Astros seize 2-0 series lead

BY BRENT ZWERNEMAN · OCT. 20, 2022

Fans and bystanders in downtown Houston skyscrapers were treated to what Minute Maid Park attendees have long been accustomed to: an Alex Bregman home run in the postseason.

Bregman's 14 postseason homers, the latest coming in a rare open-roofed Minute Maid, give him the most by a third baseman in big league annals. But that historical nugget was secondary to the import of Bregman's 14th: His third-inning, three-run pop into the Crawford Boxes gave the Astros their home runs in a 3-2 edging of the New York Yankees in Game 2 of the American League Championship Series.

Thanks to Bregman's instant offense Thursday night, the Astros clutch a 2-0 series lead heading to New York on Saturday. He in turn credited teammate Yordan Alvarez for beating out a double play the prior at-bat, putting runners on first and third for Bregman with two outs against Yankees starter Luis Severino.

"I was fortunate enough to get that at-bat because Yordan hustled down the line," Bregman said. "He plays the game hard."

So does Bregman, which is why none of his teammates were surprised he came through in a tight situation for the Astros, who are 5-0 in the postseason with three victories over the Seattle Mariners in the AL Division Series and the two against the Yankees, but none by more than two runs.

"We expect (it)," Astros reliever Bryan Abreu said of Bregman's clutch hitting. "Who knows if he's going to hit a home run or a base hit, but we just have amazing players."

Abreu teamed with Ryan Pressly to preserve the victory for Framber Valdez, who got stronger over the course of his seven innings. Valdez surrendered two runs, but if not for his fielding, he might not have surrendered any.

After Aaron Judge singled leading off the fourth, Valdez couldn't corral a dribbler off the bat of Giancarlo Stanton. Valdez made a second error on the play, throwing wildly to first base, which allowed Judge to get to third and Stanton to second. Anthony Rizzo's grounder to first scored Judge, and Stanton came home on a Gleyber Torres single.

"Back in 2019, I probably would have been done with the game. I probably would have lost all focus there at that moment," Valdez said. "But those are all things that we work on and just continue working hard on to be able to focus better and get better in the game."

Valdez indeed recovered his focus, striking out Josh Donaldson and Kyle Higashioka to preserve the 3-2 lead. The lefthander then retired nine of the 10 batters he faced in his final three innings, finishing with a flourish by striking out the side 1-2-3 in the seventh.

Abreu's eighth inning was not without adventure. After Harrison Bader walked with one out, Aaron Judge hit a laser to right field that looked like it might go out. Kyle Tucker made a leaping grab at the fence to deny the slugger whose 62 home runs this season set an American League record.

"He's the biggest dude in baseball and the most powerful guy in baseball," Astros manager Dusty Baker said of Judge. "You would rather not have to face him with any men on base, and we've escaped so far."

Abreu then fanned Stanton, and Pressly struck out three of the four batters he faced in the ninth to earn his second save in as many nights.

In winning their first five playoff games, the Astros have largely done it with the long ball. The 10 homers they have hit are responsible for 16 of their 20 postseason runs (80 percent). They are only 4-for-32 with runners in scoring position. Bregman's homer was Houston's first hit in such a situation since his eighth-inning insurance single in Game 2 of the AL Division Series.

But it was enough.

With catcher Martín Maldonado, who was hit by a pitch to start the third inning, on third and Alvarez on first with the two

OPPOSITE: With Minute Maid Park's roof open and the wind blowing out, Alex Bregman supplies sufficient launch angle to a 97.4 mph Luis Severino fastball that cleared the Crawford Boxes in left field. The three-run blast, which accounted for all the Astros' scoring, gave Bregman 14 postseason home runs, an MLB record among third basemen. He would have 15 at postseason's end. **KAREN WARREN/ HOUSTON CHRONICLE**

RIGHT: Framber Valdez exits the mound in the fifth inning after preserving the Astros' 3-2 lead by retiring New York slugger Aaron Judge on a fly ball that stranded Harrison Bader, left, at first base. Valdez lasted seven innings and struck out nine Yankees, including all three he faced in his final frame. **KAREN WARREN/HOUSTON CHRONICLE**

outs, Severino started Bregman with two 96 mph fastballs. Bregman fouled off the first and took the second for a ball.

Bregman then took a changeup for a strike before swatting a 97 mph fastball into the Crawford Boxes, touching off a raucous celebration in Minute Maid and in the taller buildings beyond the outfield fence, thanks to the unusual unobstructed view – albeit from a distance.

"Just trying to square up a ball is tough off him," Bregman said of Severino, who fell to 0-3 against the Astros in the postseason (including 2017 and 2019). "He's one of the best pitchers in the game. I missed under a few fastballs and was fortunate enough to square that one up and give us the lead."

Bregman hit .259 in the regular season but steadily improved as summer turned to fall. He is hitting .318 in the five postseason games so far, including two home runs. His two-run shot in the eighth inning o the Astros' 8-7 comeback victory over th Mariners in Game 1 of the ALDS helpe set the table for Alvarez's game-winnin three-run blast in the ninth.

Bregman, who at 13 postseason homer had been tied with Justin Turner for the all time high among third basemen, said a sligh shift in his stance this season has made a

LEFT: Astros right fielder Kyle Tucker would go through a wall for his teammates, which he didn't quite have to do in snagging an "uh oh" laser by Aaron Judge for the second out in the New York eighth. Bryan Abreu, who had walked Harrison Bader before Judge came up, ended the inning with a called strikeout of Giancarlo Stanton. BRETT COOMER/HOUSTON CHRONICLE

the difference in his swing.

"I've been landing open for (something) like two years, so I needed to fix some mechanical things," Bregman explained. "My front side was kind of flying off the baseball when I would swing. So during the All-Star break, I got into the cage and really got after it and tried to get mechanically sound."

Bregman, 28, also cited his good health as a reason for his later-season success, and Baker concurred while also praising Bregman's dogged approach to the game.

"The main thing is that he's stayed healthy and stayed in the lineup," Baker said. "That was a problem the last couple of years. ... He never really got going for a couple of years there. But this year I think he played more games than anybody, and that gave him time to get his stroke and get his legs together.

"He's been remarkable in the second half and into these playoffs. He didn't have a very good playoffs last year (hitting .217 in the ALCS and .095 in the World Series), and he's a big-game guy. He enjoys it. He's a gym rat who enjoys baseball as much as anything."

20
HOUSTON
loanDepot
POSTSEASON

Everything clicking

GM's deadline pickups contribute three RBIs as Blankees again fall victim to Cristian Javier

BY CHANDLER ROME · OCT. 22, 2022

NEW YORK — James Click did not break the bank or broker a blockbuster, foreign for a franchise that has executed each type of trade deadline deal during its golden era. The Astros general manager took a practical approach across those three days in August, careful not to disturb a culture or do anything drastic. He pondered deals that would have drawn fanfare. He brought in a bench bat and backup catcher instead.

Click didn't place a premium on winning a press conference. Trades are made with an eye toward October, when each roster spot is sacred and selflessness shines. Houston's clubhouse calls itself a family, one strengthened across six seasons of scorn, success and the pursuit of perfection. Entering it is not a simple task. Everyday players elsewhere can become part-time contributors to Houston's perpetual success. Egos are unwelcome, or at least eradicated at the door.

"We didn't have the greatest culture in 2016," Lance McCullers Jr. said Saturday. "We got guys like Brian McCann, Carlos Beltrán, and they let us know we're here to win. We're here to create a family in this clubhouse. It's not about hazing guys. It's not about giving guys a hard time or making guys earn their stripes. If you're wearing this uniform, you're one of us — if you've been here one day, been here 20 years. We're going to laugh, be happy, smile, and we're going to show up every day ready to play. And I think we need to have that mindset that makes everyone equals — it doesn't matter how much money you make. And I think it's worked here."

Six consecutive American League Championship Series appearances are the result. A 5-0 win Saturday at Yankee Stadium put the team a victory away from its fourth pennant in the same time frame. Turnover is constant, and the culture survives, even now when players put on a jersey and become pariahs for a scandal in which they did not participate. Not everyone can embrace life like this. This August, Click asked Trey Mancini and Christian Vázquez to try.

Championship clubs, Click contended, shouldn't have cavernous holes to address. His did not. The best additions he could make were on the margins, two men to lengthen his lineup, afford manager Dusty Baker more in-game maneuverability, and maintain the attitude aiding Houston's ascension into an American League dynasty. Mancini and Vázquez fulfilled Click's foremost objective. Their assimilation into Houston's culture is apparent. Saturday, they helped put this Astros club within one win of a pennant.

Mancini and Vázquez teamed to chase home three of Houston's five runs. Vázquez caught a three-hit shutout from six Houston hurlers in his first start since Oct. 2. Benched during the first two games of this series and still hitless this postseason, Mancini chased home a huge insurance run in the sixth and catalyzed Gerrit Cole's exit from the game.

"Coming into today, I woke up, and we have a 2-0 lead in the ALCS," Mancini said. "Whether I hit 1.000 in my time here or struggle a little bit like I have lately, we're in the same position. Rather than have any self-pity or feel sorry for myself, every at-bat (and) every game from here on out is going to be the biggest at-bat and game I play in my life. I'd be remiss to not wash everything in the past and put my best foot forward. That's why I was traded here — to try to help this team win a World Series."

Mancini played every day in Baltimore. Vázquez had long cemented himself as Boston's everyday catcher. Click acquired them to play part-time, provide an offensive punch, and balance a top-heavy batting order. Neither man objected to a reduced role.

"We want great people here," catcher Martín Maldonado said. "We don't want selfish players. All we want (them to do) is whatever we need to do to win games. That's the most

OPPOSITE: Make a mistake, as New York did in the second inning of Game 3, and the Astros will capitalize. After reaching with two outs when center fielder Harrison Bader dropped his fly ball, Christian Vázquez had a cheerful greeting at the plate for Chas McCormick, who gave the Astros a 2-0 lead with an opposite-field homer to right off Yankees ace Gerrit Cole, to the dismay of catcher Jose Trevino.
KAREN WARREN/HOUSTON CHRONICLE

RIGHT: Astros righthander Cristian Javier, who threw seven no-hit innings at Yankee Stadium in a June 25 start, allowed only one hit, a fourth-inning double by Giancarlo Stanton, in Game 3. Javier lasted 5 1/3 scoreless innings, striking out five and walking three. **KAREN WARREN/HOUSTON CHRONICLE**

important thing. We haven't got selfish players. Whoever is coming here is willing to be like us, and that's why the culture doesn't change."

For two months, neither Vázquez nor Mancini accomplished what Click envisioned, garnering warranted criticism. Vázquez had a .585 OPS in 35 games after the trade. Mancini lost feel for his lower-body mechanics and faded in September. The .535 OPS he posted that month left him almost unplayable.

Baker went back to him for Game 3 of the ALCS due to familiarity. Mancini played the first four months of this season in the American League East. So did Vázquez. Few in Houston's clubhouse had more experience against the Yankees' pitching staff — or facing it at Yankee Stadium. Saturday exploited that.

"It's easier. I've been here in 2018 (with the Red Sox). We won (a World Series)," Vázquez said. "We won two games here in the LDS, and I think it was easier knowing the way the fans go about their business."

Vázquez caught another nine-inning assault against a hapless New York offense. The Yankees are now 12-for-94 with 41 strikeouts across these three games. On the rare occasion they mounted a rally, Vázquez vanquished it. His fifth-inning throw nabbed Harrison Bader trying to steal second base and erased Cristian Javier's leadoff walk.

Vázquez and Javier work seamlessly together. Baker did not want to separate Maldonado from Justin Verlander or Framber Valdez during the series' first two games, relegating Vázquez to a reserve role.

"When they put me out there, I'm going to do my job," Vázquez said. "I don't control that. I'm here for my team and my teammates and ready all the time."

In his first start since Oct. 1, Javier struck out five across 5 1/3 excellent innings. Eleven consecutive Yankees could not muster a hit against him to begin Saturday's game, inviting wonder whether Javier could author another bid for history. He spun seven hitless innings at this ballpark on June 25 before Héctor Neris and Ryan Pressly procured the final six outs of the franchise's 14th no-hitter.

LEFT: As general manager of a team with no glaring flaws, James Click didn't need to make a big splash at the Aug. 2 trade deadline, although he did add reinforcements in catcher Christian Vázquez, first baseman/outfielder Trey Mancini and lefthanded reliever Will Smith. Hired by Houston in 2020 from the Tampa Bay Rays, with whom he was vice president of baseball operations, Click presided over an Astros franchise that progressed from that year's American League Championship Series to the 2021 AL pennant to the 2022 World Series title. **BRETT COOMER/HOUSTON CHRONICLE**

Giancarlo Stanton spared his team from the shame with a fourth-inning double. The Yankees notched just two more hits, singles by Matt Carpenter and Bader off Bryan Abreu with two outs in the ninth. Houston allowed the leadoff man aboard twice in nine innings, neutralizing a New York lineup that refused to assist Cole.

The Yankees ace seemed a man all alone Saturday. None of the 25 men around him appeared willing or able to provide any resistance to the Astros' continued onslaught.

Cole, who left the Astros as a free agent after they won the 2019 AL pennant, is paid handsomely, but even he needs help. Bader dropped Vázquez's two-out fly ball in the second inning, forcing Cole to face a batter he never should have. Chas McCormick poked his 98 mph fastball onto the short porch in right field, affording Houston's dominant pitching staff the only cushion it needed.

Cole started the sixth inning with a two-run deficit still intact. Alex Bregman crushed a changeup for an opposite-field double. Yuli Gurriel blooped a single. A walk to Kyle Tucker in between helped load the bases and ended Cole's evening. Manager Aaron Boone cited Mancini's "good at-bats against him already" as the impetus for his change. Mancini crushed a fly ball to the center-field warning track in the second and worked a six-pitch walk against Cole in the fourth.

Boone asked Lou Trivino to try to tame him. Mancini struck the sixth pitch he saw to left field for a sacrifice fly, offering insurance for a pitching staff that threw most of this series without any. Vázquez stepped in seeking more. He sat on a slider from Trivino and took it into left field. Two runs scored before Vázquez reached first base. He turned toward his dugout and started to celebrate — an October rite of passage Houston's two new players spent Saturday embracing.

"This is a different animal than anything I've ever played in to this point in my career. It's what we've all dreamed of our whole lives, and it's fun," Mancini said. "You'd be remiss not to enjoy it and go about it the right way rather than be overly nervous or not want the spotlight."

Normally a playoff stalwart, Jose Altuve had taken a licking at the plate, setting an MLB record by going hitless in his first 25 at-bats of the postseason. He got off the schneid in the fifth inning, poking a double to right field off former Astros teammate Gerrit Cole. **BRETT COOMER/HOUSTON CHRONICLE**

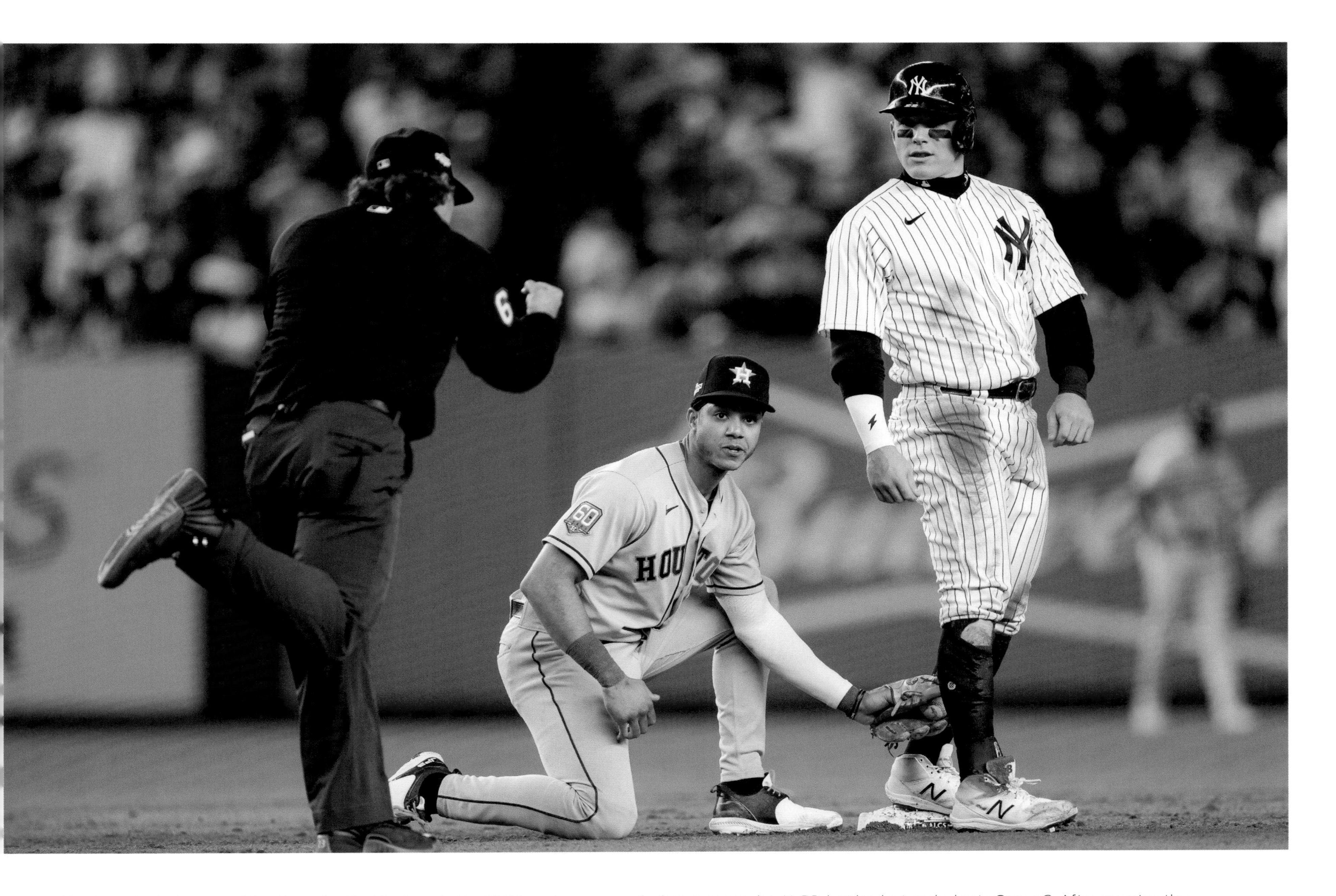

Harrison Bader homered five times for the Yankees in the 2022 postseason, including twice in the ALCS, but had a tough day in Game 3. After opening the door to two Astros runs with his second-inning drop in center field, Bader was rung up by second-base umpire Chris Guccione on an attempted steal in the fourth. Shortstop Jeremy Peña applied the tag, thanks to an assist from catcher Christian Vázquez. **BRETT COOMER/HOUSTON CHRONICLE**

ALCS GAME 4 // ASTROS 6, YANKEES 5

Culture club

Some faces have changed during the Astros' golden era, but with sweep of Yankees, the winning continues unabated

BY CHANDLER ROME · OCT. 23, 2022

NEW YORK — The Astros shed a superstar each winter and still find the same fate every fall. Their homogeneity is the envy of an entire league still trying to keep pace. Scandal threatened to scar this franchise but only strengthened its resolve. Faces change and voices differ, but the aura is abiding: a brand of baseball that transcends one or two individuals, ignores invective and erases — or exceeds — any outside expectations.

Teams aren't conditioned to absorb the defections Houston endures. The Astros defy convention. Before them, no American League franchise had reached six consecutive League Championship Series. The first team in the run featured a core containing homegrown faces hailed as the future. The latest came sans George Springer or Carlos Correa and at Gerrit Cole's expense. Their replacements coalesced with the remaining core to put this team on the precipice of another championship.

"It's culture, man. We embrace the new ones," bench coach Joe Espada said. "The love for each other, the commitment to our work, the purpose. We know exactly what we want to do. We come in from day one to be the last team standing, and that's what we try to do every year."

On Sunday night, the Astros reminded baseball of their staying power. This team bears only a slight resemblance to its recent brethren but finds itself with the same opportunity. A 6-5 victory at Yankee Stadium handed the Astros their fourth pennant in six seasons. Four wins against the Philadelphia Phillies separate Houston from its second World Series title.

The first is now five years old, too aged for a franchise that has raised its standards. Owner Jim Crane's demands exceed pennants, perhaps a catalyst of this team's continued dominance. A sign-stealing scandal sullied the 2017 trophy to most, but not those who earned it. A core of five remains to receive the vitriol and maintain a mindset.

Jose Altuve, Alex Bregman, Yuli Gurriel, Lance McCullers Jr. and Justin Verlander are the lone constants across all four pennants, although McCullers (2019) and Verlander (2021) each missed one of the seasons because of injury. Their guidance cannot be overstated, nor can their ability to further a culture cultivated across the organization.

"I think the core group that we have and that we've kept are absolute difference-makers," hitting coach Troy Snitker said. "They make people around them better. They welcome in our new players, and they get them up to a level that's on par with what we expect."

They realized it while eight outs away from their first October defeat in 2022. Mistakes are this club's friend. Names and faces do not change that. Give the Astros a crack, and they'll break everything open. Yankees second baseman Gleyber Torres tested the theory in the seventh inning, with his team nursing a rare lead.

With New York up 5-4, Torres fielded Jeremy Peña's one-out ground ball, turned toward second and threw it into left field. Altuve, whose hustle had produced an infield single by the thinnest of margins, scurried safely into scoring position as the tying run. Peña sprinted through first, forcing reliever Jonathan Loáisiga to face a man he never should have. Yordan Alvarez struck the next pitch he threw for a tying single. Bregman followed with another single to put the Astros up 6-5.

Altuve and Peña both scored, affording baseball's best bullpen a lead it had no problem protecting, sealing a pennant that long felt foregone. Houston held a four-month residence atop the American League, staking its place following four June games in this very ballpark.

Pundits once hailed this Yankees club as the greatest in the franchise's storied history.

OPPOSITE: An Astros mainstay since his MLB debut on Aug. 21, 2016, Cuban first baseman Yuli Gurriel puts the Astros ahead 4-3 with an RBI single capping their four-run third. The American League batting champion in 2021, when he hit .319, the 38-year-old Gurriel struggled to a .242/.288/.360 slash line in 2022. But he came alive in the playoffs, going 6-for-15 (.400) with a home run in the ALDS and 5-for-15 (.333) with another homer in the ALCS. BRETT COOMER/HOUSTON CHRONICLE

RIGHT: Starter Lance McCullers Jr. battled his way through five innings in the Astros' ALCS clincher, surrendering three runs, eight hits and a walk while throwing 100 pitches over five innings. And he was pleased to end the fifth with his sixth strikeout, freezing rookie Oswaldo Cabrera with a slider to preserve a 4-3 lead.
BRETT COOMER/HOUSTON CHRONICLE

The Astros arrived around midseason and made a mockery of them. Two Aaron Judge walk-offs spared New York from a four-game sweep in early summer. In that series, the Yankees did not throw a pitch with a lead, instilling a foreign feeling inside the Bronx. Intimidation is king in this city.

The Astros fear no one. Deficits and derision do nothing to deter them, defining the chasm between these two franchises. Altuve, Alvarez and Kyle Tucker finished 8-for-43 during these four ALCS games. Houston won all of them, relying upon Bregman, Peña and Chas McCormick to propel its offense. Peña stepped into Correa's shoes at shortstop. McCormick replaced Springer in center.

"It's a stroke of luck, and it's a little bit about high-character guys coming here and playing unbelievable," McCullers said. "Guys keep stepping up, are the best versions of themselves, and we find ourselves in the World Series."

Judge went 1-for-16 in this four-game sweep. Without the American League's home run king, New York could not function, nor could it handle any bit of prosperity, including a three-run uprising against McCullers.

Two delays could have marred McCullers' start before it began. The team gave him an extra day of rest after an errant champagne bottle banged into his elbow during Houston's clubhouse celebration in the Division Series. McCullers characterized the injury as a bone bruise and brushed aside any long-term concern. A 90-minute weather delay Sunday provided another impediment.

McCullers surrendered eight hits and four runs in five innings. A baserunner reached in four of the five frames he finished. He needed 100 pitches to procure 15 outs. New York's batting order featured seven righthanded hitters, making it mandatory for McCullers to harness his slider to neutralize them. He failed. McCullers spun 36 sliders across his five-inning outing. The Yankees swung and missed against two of them.

"My stuff was actually pretty good. The Yankees were tough on me. I was looking back at the board because it has all the movement, and I'm like, 'That's good pitches,'" McCullers said. "They're just tough, bro. You can't hold down a good team forever. They're at home (and) do not want to get swept or lose."

LEFT: Game 2 hero Alex Bregman comes through again, putting the Astros up 6-5 with a seventh-inning RBI single off Clay Holmes, who had just entered Game 4 for the Yankees. Previous batter Yordan Alvarez had tied the game with a single off Jonathan Loáisiga. **BRETT COOMER/HOUSTON CHRONICLE**

Hope carried New York, which held a 3-0 lead after two innings thanks to RBI hits by Giancarlo Stanton, Torres and Anthony Rizzo, only so far. Tasked on Sunday with saving the Yankees' season, southpaw Nestor Cortes never appeared comfortable. He slogged through two scoreless innings with imprecise command, disadvantageous counts and constant traffic.

Houston stranded two baserunners against him across the first two frames. The third inning invited alarm. Velocity plummeted across Cortes' entire repertoire. His four-seam fastball did not reach 90 mph after averaging 92 in the first two frames.

Cortes walked just 2.2 batters per nine innings during the regular season. He almost exceeded his average in the third inning alone, starting it with free passes to Martín Maldonado and Altuve. Manager Aaron Boone brought a trainer to visit Cortes during Altuve's at-bat. Cortes remained in the game after a brief discussion. Altuve worked his walk, putting Peña at the plate.

Peña is the archetype of this franchise's continuity. Houston allowed Correa to walk last winter and made this rookie its starting shortstop. Peña bypassed Class AA and played 30 games at Class AAA before making his major league debut in April. Replacing a cornerstone with a novice brings no guarantees.

"We have grown this culture to spread around the clubhouse and the entire minor league system," Espada said. "So when the guys get up here, they know they belong. They know they can do it."

Perhaps this is what other franchises can't comprehend. Peña immersed himself into a clubhouse that embraced him. He struggled in the second half but never lost the faith of the veterans six or seven years his senior. He finished this series 6-for-18 to win MVP honors. His crowning moment came when Cortes hung a slider. Peña pulverized it into the seats for game-tying three-run homer, and a rite of October repeated itself.

"They take care of each other, and every year we're able to bounce back and get here," Crane said. "It's an unbelievable run, and I'm extremely proud of what they've been able to accomplish."

enjoy the show.
POSTSEASON
ALCS

Rookie? Hah!

Producing beyond his years, Jeremy Peña captures series MVP award

BY DANIELLE LERNER · OCT. 23, 2022

NEW YORK — Dreams are born and die in the month when baseball is played under the darkest skies and direst conditions. Breathless cruelty and unimaginable joy exist on either side of a razor's edge. October baseball does not discriminate between battle-scarred legends and doe-eyed newcomers.

In the win that secured another World Series appearance for the Astros, an ace pitching in his seventh career close-out playoff game fell into a three-run hole and was rescued by a rookie learning to crave October limelight.

Jeremy Peña knows about dreams because he is living his.

For six months after his big league debut, he contended with enormous expectations and appeared impervious. For four pivotal postseason games against a baseball juggernaut, no moment seemed too overwhelming.

A hostile ballpark filled with New Yorkers hoping their team could stave off elimination rooted against Peña on Sunday night. He defied them. Peña mashed a game-tying three-run homer 408 feet to left field and punctuated it with a bat flip. As he rounded third base, he looked in the direction of the Astros dugout and shrugged with both palms facing upward, as if to ask, "What are you gonna do about it?"

"It just came out," he said later.

Peña is not an exhibitionist or a showboat by nature, but the celebration felt suitable for a swing that catalyzed a Game 4 comeback that gave the Astros a sweep of the Yankees in the American League Championship Series and led the rookie shortstop to be crowned series Most Valuable Player.

Shortly after he accepted the MVP trophy on the field after the Astros' 6-5 win at Yankee Stadium, Peña embraced his girlfriend and took her phone to FaceTime his parents, who were at home in Rhode Island. Peña's mother, Carmen Cecilia, is the inspiration for the heart sign he flashes with his hands when he gets on base. His father, Geronimo, is a former St. Louis Cardinals second baseman.

"I can't wait to get them on the phone," Peña said, before adding with a smirk, "They should be here right now, but they don't love me enough."

He was joking, but there was no shortage of love directed his way Sunday. The Astros started a chant of "JP! JP!" as Peña lifted the hardware anointing him the most prized player on a dynastic team stocked with All-Stars, Gold Glovers, batting title holders and World Series champions. Peña cannot match their accolades yet, but he has been welcomed with open arms in a clubhouse of men who strive to balance selflessness with perfection.

"Such a special young kid," Astros pitcher Lance McCullers Jr. said. "Such an amazing infielder (and) teammate. He's blossoming into a silent leader for us. Just plays his heart out. Whether it was him hitting the homers or whether it was him getting on base to get to the homers, this postseason has been his."

The Yankee Stadium blast was Peña's third home run of the postseason, the first two of which were solo shots. His first delivered the Astros a series-clinching win over Seattle in the 18th inning of ALDS Game 3. His second scored the Astros' final run in a Game 1 victory over the Yankees.

His third, though, perhaps most violently altered the trajectory of a game.

McCullers started on the mound for the Astros in Game 4, and it became immediately clear he was not in possession of his best stuff. The Yankees scored two runs before he recorded two outs. They added a third in the second inning, endangering Houston's chance at a sweep.

But in the third inning, New York starter Nestor Cortes, struggling through a groin injury, issued consecutive walks to Martín Maldonado and Jose Altuve. That brought Peña to the plate as the tying run. He banished a 3-1 pitch into the stands and sparked his team back to life.

"I was like, 'Bailed me out on that one,'" McCullers said, laughing.

Peña is among five rookies in MLB history to homer in multiple series-clinching games within the same postseason. In his seven-game playoff career, he is batting .303 (10-for-33) with a .991 OPS.

OPPOSITE: Not that he was being flippant toward the partisan crowd at Yankee Stadium, but Jeremy Peña had reason to be joyous after crushing a game-tying three-run homer off Nestor Cortes in the third inning of the Astros' ALCS clincher.
KAREN WARREN/HOUSTON CHRONICLE

RIGHT: Flanked by manager Dusty Baker and TBS reporter Lauren Shehadi, who mimicked the "What are you gonna do about it?" pose he flashed toward the Astros dugout while rounding third on his Game 4 homer, rookie shortstop Jeremy Peña accepts his ALCS Most Valuable Player trophy. In the Astros' four-game sweep of the Yankees, Peña was 6-for-17 (.353) with two homers, two doubles, three runs and four RBIs.
BRETT COOMER/HOUSTON CHRONICLE

"If I start talking about him," Altuve said before Sunday's game, "we might be here two hours."

In a series that saw the Astros stifle the Yankees' Aaron Judge, Peña was their executioner. He went 6-for-17 with four RBIs, two homers, three runs and two doubles. And that included his 0-for-5 line in Game 3. His OPS against New York was 1.177.

To call Peña's October performance a breakout doesn't do justice to the remarkable regular season he authored. He tied for first among major league shortstops in defensive runs saved, hit 22 home runs, and is a finalist for the Gold Glove Award at shortstop. The Astros knew what Peña, 25, was capable of by the time the postseason rolled around. So did opposing teams, though they have been powerless to stop him.

What Peña's playoff prowess has done, however, is hasten a conclusion many deemed inevitable. The Astros are going to their fourth World Series in the last six years absent Carlos Correa, the former franchise shortstop who got them to the previous three, but with a rookie replacement who is fast solidifying his own place in Houston lore.

"We weren't expecting that," Astros first-base coach Omar López said. "We were expecting a guy that is gonna be good, but not that good. It looked like Jeremy, toward the end of the season, built up his confidence and played in the playoffs like he's been in the big leagues forever."

Astros players and coaches laud Peña for his maturity and work ethic. Perhaps the biggest proof of both is the adjustment he made in the season's final month, with guidance from the team's hitting coaches, to fix his trouble hitting sliders and high-spin pitches.

The Mariners and Yankees identified that as Peña's weakness and attempted to exploit

LEFT: Their ALCS sweep made the Astros the ninth franchise to win four pennants within six seasons or less. With their 40 American League flags, the Yankees have accomplished the feat in more combinations than bear listing. The other teams to do it: the Cubs (1906–08, 1910), Athletics (1910–11, 1913–14), Giants (1921–24), Cardinals (twice, 1926, 1928, 1930–31 and 1942–44, 1946), Dodgers (1952–53, 1955–56), Orioles (1966, 1969–71) and Braves (1991–92, 1995–96). BRETT COOMER/HOUSTON CHRONICLE

it. He did not let them, Astros hitting coach Troy Snitker explained.

"He made the pitchers second-guess the game plan," Snitker said. "He started covering a lot of different stuff. I think going into this series, both series, teams thought they could just spin him, and he showed that he was gonna be ready for it. And it turned into a tough game plan and a tough out."

In Sunday's seventh inning, with Altuve on first and the Astros trailing 5-4, Peña grounded into a fielder's choice at second base, but Gleyber Torres' throwing error allowed both Astros runners to remain safely aboard. After Yordan Alvarez's RBI single, Alex Bregman's soft-contact RBI single chased Peña home from third base.

Immediately after he crossed the plate to give the Astros a one-run lead, Peña helped protect it with his defense. Anthony Rizzo was responsible for the Yankees' two biggest run-scoring hits of the game, an RBI double and a game-tying single. He arrived at the plate to lead off the seventh inning against Bryan Abreu and struck a ground ball against the shift through the right side of the infield.

Running to his left from behind second base, Peña scooped the ball off the grass and in one fluid motion unleashed a spinning throw to first base for the out.

Thirty minutes later, he was lifting a trophy and cementing his part in a dynasty that refuses to die.

"It's surreal," he said. "You dream about this stuff when you're a kid. And shout-out to my teammates. We show up every single day. We stayed true to ourselves all year. We're a step away from our ultimate goal."

POSTSEASON

OPPOSITE: How could the Astros not embrace their fourth postseason elimination of the Yankees in eight seasons? The 2022 American League Championship Series sweep followed triumphs in the 2015 AL wild card game, 2017 ALCS and 2019 ALCS, much to the delight of, from left, Héctor Neris, Cristian Javier, Jose Altuve and Justin Verlander. **BRETT COOMER/HOUSTON CHRONICLE**

LEFT: In his 25th season of major league managing, Dusty Baker had his sights set on his first World Series crown. He fell short after piloting the 2002 Giants and 2021 Astros to the Fall Classic. In 19 years as an MLB player, Baker won one ring in three World Series tries with the Dodgers, who captured the 1981 championship over the Yankees after losing to them in 1977 and 1978. **BRETT COOMER/HOUSTON CHRONICLE**

BELOW FAR LEFT: Justin Verlander, who turned in a model pitching performance to earn the victory in Game 1, celebrates the fifth pennant in Astros history with wife Kate Upton. **BRETT COOMER/HOUSTON CHRONICLE**

BELOW LEFT: Say it and spray it! The Astros are 2022 American League champions, to which catcher Martín Maldonado testifies in the visitors' clubhouse at Yankee Stadium. **KAREN WARREN/HOUSTON CHRONICLE**

GURRIEL
10
HOUSTON
ASTROS

WORLD SERIES GAME 1 // PHILLIES 6, ASTROS 5

Off the rails

ustin Verlander blows early 5-run lead; .T. Realmuto delivers crushing 10th-inning blow

Y CHANDLER ROME · OCT. 28, 2022

Bat met ball, and Kyle Tucker flipped his lumber, swagger from a player who rely exudes it. As he watched the baseball sappear into the Astros' bullpen, a crowd 42,903 broke into bedlam.

"We Want Houston," the folks began to ellow, mimicking New York Yankees fans ho chanted something similar before the merican League Championship Series.

The Astros authored a methodical four-game veep to silence them. Presumptions of another ppeared on the horizon. Tucker's three-run omer, which made him the first Astro to go eep twice in a World Series game, staked ne of this generation's greatest pitchers to a ve-run advantage. Not since July 26, 2021, ad Houston lost a game it led by five runs, a pan of 65 consecutive comfortable cushions.

Baseball promises nothing. One bounce bobble can break hearts or build statues. uarantees are few, even with a pitcher who pitomizes excellence.

"I feel really confident that 99 percent the time that I'm able to hold that lead," ustin Verlander said.

On the one stage he cannot conquer, erlander could not. He is a future Hall of amer whose World Series failures reached nadir on a nightmarish Friday night at Iinute Maid Park.

Verlander gave away the Astros' five-run lead and allowed the Philadelphia Phillies to wrestle home-field advantage from the American League champions. Verlander made his eighth Fall Classic start and now sports a 6.07 ERA. No pitcher with at least 30 World Series innings has a higher one.

This year's Game 1 delivered perhaps the most perplexing chapter of this catastrophic Fall Classic storybook. Verlander vacillated from untouchable to unwatchable in an instant, aided by an abnormally long leash from manager Dusty Baker.

Verlander imploded in the sort of inglorious fashion he hardly ever shows, sending Houston to a crushing 6-5, extra-inning loss at Minute Maid Park.

"I need to do better. No excuses," Verlander said. "I felt like I had some guys in good situations and just wasn't able to quite make the pitches that I wanted to."

Baseball's best bullpen tried for four innings to buoy its ace. A fifth turned fatal. Baker eschewed convention and turned to a converted starter, one who sparkled in Seattle but slipped up Friday. On the sixth pitch he threw in the 10th inning, Luis Garcia surrendered what proved to be a game-winning home run to Phillies catcher J.T. Realmuto, whose opposite-field shot to right was out of Tucker's reach.

"Honestly, I thought I got enough of it," Realmuto said, "but I kind of had flashbacks of the play that Tucker made on (Aaron) Judge's ball that last series (in Game 2 of the ALCS), and once I saw him running back to the wall, I was thinking in my head, 'Oh, please just don't catch it. Just don't catch it.' I knew it was going to be close. I thought originally I had enough, but once I saw him running back to the wall, I wasn't so sure."

Realmuto, who has caught every inning for the Phillies this postseason, became the first catcher to hit a World Series home run in extras since Carlton Fisk's Game 6 walk-off for the Red Sox against the Reds in 1975.

"It's pretty incredible, honestly," Realmuto said. "But for me, it's so cool to see the way this team is playing. It's been a different hero every single night. It's been that way all postseason long."

Citing the team's "matchup sheet," Baker started the 10th with Garcia over Ryne Stanek, who posted a 1.15 ERA in the regular season to set an Astros record for a reliever but had pitched just twice this postseason. Stanek relieved Garcia to finish the 10th.

"That was the deciding run, but we had the winning runs on base to end the game," Baker said.

OPPOSITE: After cruising through three innings and being staked to a 5-0 lead in Game 1 against the Phillies, Astros pitcher Justin Verlander, right, needed a talking-to in the fourth from catcher Martín Maldonado, from left, pitching coach Josh Miller and first baseman Yuli Gurriel. The mound visit was preceded by a walk to Phillies shortstop Bryson Stott, one batter after Alec Bohm made it a 5-3 game with a two-run double. Verlander induced an inning-ending popup but found more trouble in the fifth. By night's end, he was 0-6 with a 6.07 ERA in eight career World Series starts. **KAREN WARREN/HOUSTON CHRONICLE**

RIGHT: With Kyle Tucker really in the swing of things, the Astros got off to a promising start in Game 1. After beginning the scoring with a solo home run off Aaron Nola in the second inning, Tucker watches his three-run shot against the Phillies ace take flight in the third, putting Houston up 5-0 and making Tucker the first Astro to go deep twice in a World Series game. **KAREN WARREN/HOUSTON CHRONICLE**

In the Houston 10th, Alex Bregman doubled with one out off David Robertson, who then struck out Tucker before walking Yuli Gurriel. A wild pitch moved the runners to second and third, but Aledmys Díaz grounded out to end a game it looked like Houston might win an inning earlier.

In the bottom of the ninth, Jose Altuve singled off Seranthony Dominguez with two outs, then stole second. Jeremy Peña lofted a flare to right field that looked like it would drop before Nick Castellanos sped in for a sliding catch to keep the game tied at 5.

"I thought it was hit so softly that I didn't think he was going to get there," Realmuto said. "I thought the game was over. But then I saw him charging in, coming in hot, and I thought, 'Oh, man. He might have a chance to catch that.' … That play was huge. You can't say enough about it."

Castellanos felt confident from the get-go. It helped that he had positioned himself slightly shallower after Altuve's steal.

"I just thought Peña had a better chance of trying to bloop something in there than torching something over my head. So that was kind of my thought process there," Castellanos said. "I felt like I read the swing pretty well, and as soon as I saw the direction of the ball, I felt like I got a good jump on it."

Castellanos' catch helped continue what has become an Astros-Phillies postseason tradition dating to 1980. In that year's best-of-five National League Championship Series, which Houston lost 3-2 in heartbreaking fashion, the last four games required extra innings.

In the teams' first postseason matchup since that one, Baker and Astros pitching coach Josh Miller deployed a far more lax approach than Phillies manager Rob Thomson, who decisive deployed five relievers — including presump tive Game 3 starter Ranger Suárez for two ou across the seventh and eighth.

The Philadelphia quintet quieted an Astr offense that ambushed Phillies ace Aaron Nol Thomson was quick to remove his starter wit one out in the fifth, calling on lefthander Jo Alvarado to face Yordan Alvarez and Tucker th third time through the order.

"I think once we scored the three (in th fourth to make it 5-3), you were kind of feelin it," Thomson said. "Like, OK, we got back

LEFT: Philadelphia fans could have dubbed their right fielder Nick "Of Time" Castellanos after he saved the game for the Phillies with a magnificent sliding catch on Jeremy Peña's flare to end the ninth. Jose Altuve, who had singled with two outs and stolen second base, would easily have scored a tiebreaking run had the ball fallen in. BRETT COOMER/HOUSTON CHRONICLE

ıis thing; now the momentum's changed. And ıat's really why I went to Alvarado in the fifth ıning, which I haven't done all year. Because I ıought that the momentum change there was ›important to keep. Get through those guys, ıd we'll figure out the rest later."

Philadelphia's relievers threw 5 2/3 score-ss innings from there, but regardless, one ıdisputable fact endures: Houston handed a ıture Hall of Famer a five-run lead and lost.

"If you would have told me we'd score five ıns off Aaron Nola with the way he looked ıring the series at the end of the regular season (when the righthander threw 6 2/3 innings in a 3-0 win at Minute Maid Park that secured Philadelphia's wild card berth), I'd have said, 'Yeah, we're in good shape,'" Miller said. "But ultimately let it get away from us a little bit today."

It escaped almost in an instant, an incredible decline after Verlander's dominant start. He retired the first nine Phillies he saw. Six of them faced either an 0-2 or 1-2 count. Verlander commanded his entire repertoire and worked with a wonderful pace, plowing through a powerful Philadelphia lineup almost without pause.

Bryce Harper tried to create one in the second inning, stepping out of the batter's box after swinging through two elevated four-seam fastballs. Verlander remained on the rubber throughout Harper's timeout, refusing to participate in the mind games. Harper returned, and Verlander fired a 95.2 mph fastball to finish him, the sort of display that portends dominance.

Verlander needed 36 pitches to procure his first nine outs. None of the first 10 Phillies to face him reached base. Verlander generated six swings and misses during that span. He received three against the final 13 Phillies he faced. Eight of them reached, starting with Rhys Hoskins' one-out single in the fourth as Philadelphia got its second look at Houston's ace.

"You've seen it once, so there's some familiarity there," Thomson said. "I think that's why we had some success off him the second time. But I thought the at-bats were really good. We got his pitch count up pretty good. I thought his stuff was good. But we had some good at-bats."

RIGHT: Though willing to go above and beyond, Astros right fielder Kyle Tucker was unable to reach J.T. Realmuto's tiebreaking home run ball off Luis Garcia in the 10th. **BRETT COOMER/HOUSTON CHRONICLE**

Verlander needed 36 pitches to procure his first nine outs. He required 54 to secure the next six. His command disappeared, and he could not land either of his breaking balls for strikes. Philadelphia pounded some poorly executed sliders and curveballs for crucial hits.

"A lot of mistakes over the heart of the plate to good hitters, the hard part of the lineup. We didn't execute pitches, and we got burned," Astros catcher Martín Maldonado said. "When you don't execute pitches against good hitters, they're not going to miss them."

Philadelphia still gave Verlander a chance to escape. After Hoskins' single in the fourth, Realmuto struck a two-strike slider straight back to Verlander. Hoskins strayed too far off first base on contact. Verlander caught the baseball on a line but dropped it while rushing to turn an inning-ending double play. He settled for only the out at first retiring Realmuto, affording hope to a lineup that thrives on any whiff of it.

The next four Phillies reached base. Harper and Castellanos each struck subpar sliders for singles. Castellanos' blooper brought Hoskins home from third, scrapping any thought of a shutout. After Castellanos' hit, Verlander committed perhaps his most massive mistake: hanging a first-pitch curveball against Alec Bohm. Bohm destroyed it into the left-field corner for a bases-clearing double, trimmin Houston's lead to two and tampering the par beginning in the ballpark.

"I wasn't executing pitches as well Verlander said. "They got some traffic on th bases and managed to have some really goo at-bats and put the ball in play. I feel like needed to execute a little bit better."

Aces are afforded a longer leash, but in th fifth, Baker reacted far too slowly to Verlander

LEFT: Philadelphia's J.T. Realmuto, who had tied Game 1 with a two-run double in the fifth, receives kudos from teammate Bryce Harper (8) after becoming the first catcher to hit an extra-inning home run in the World Series since Boston's Carlton Fisk against Cincinnati in Game 6 of the 1975 Fall Classic. The Phillies' 6-5 victory marked only the sixth time a team overcame a deficit of five runs or more to win a World Series game. **BRETT COOMER/HOUSTON CHRONICLE**

nraveling. Brandon Marsh began the inning ith a double before Verlander walked Kyle chwarber. No one stirred in Houston's bullpen.

"It's hard to take Justin out, because he can ruggle for a while, but he usually gets it back gether," Baker said. "You don't want to just ͻ through your whole bullpen that early in ıe game."

Houston possesses an embarrassment of itching riches. Baker did not act like it. He can afford to be aggressive because of the depth accrued in this bullpen. Verlander's pedigree prevented his manager from doing it. Bryan Abreu did not begin to throw until Hoskins hit a fly to shortstop for the first out of the fifth. Realmuto, reaffirming his position not only as baseball's best defensive backstop but offensive catcher as well, hammered a two-run double to tie the game.

Baker did not budge. Harper and Castellanos loomed for a third look at Houston's languishing ace. Harper bounced out, advancing the go-ahead run to third base for Castellanos. Verlander supplied five pitches, the final a wicked curveball that finally received a chase.

Verlander shuffled from the mound following the strikeout, perhaps his final act as an Astro. The 39-year-old is expected to exercise the opt-out in his contract and test free agency this winter. For three innings, Friday featured all the circumstances for one final coronation. Instead, it became another Fall Classic catastrophe.

"This team, we have an ability when our backs (are) against the wall to play our best baseball," Verlander said. "And I expect nothing different moving forward from everybody in this locker room, including myself. And hopefully, I get another opportunity to pitch and can do better."

ASTROS
WORLD SERIES
Wilson
10
3

WORLD SERIES GAME 2 // ASTROS 5, PHILLIIES 2

Affirmation of an ace

3uoyed by his sports psychologist, Framber Valdez evens series with a gem

Y CHANDLER ROME · OCT. 29, 2002

At the barbershop before the biggest start of his life, Framber Valdez followed ıe plan that put him here: on the precipice f acehood and with the trust of a team eetering toward a two-game World Series eficit. He phoned the sports psychologist ho mended his mind and must still remind im to breathe when baseball threatens to etray him.

"Remember this," Dr. Andy Nuñez told is prized pupil. "Just focus on the routine e worked on."

Valdez's pre-start routine is not complete ithout this one call. For the past three easons, Nuñez nurtured Valdez's wayward oirit and stabilized a career careening in the rong direction. Stuff has never been Valdez's ıortcoming. Scattered thoughts prevented im from throwing it with any consistency.

It took two seasons for Valdez to seek elp and three more to put it into practice n baseball's biggest stage. He surrendered 0 earned runs and secured 14 outs during wo World Series starts last season.

"My emotions got the best of me," Valdez aid through an interpreter. "I wasn't able to ırow even more than two innings without iving up a run. But those were things that was able to learn: Separate my emotions om my job being on the field. Whenever m on the field, on the mound, I just keep my emotions outside of the field (and) try to stay calm, collected."

The two-start disaster sullied an otherwise sterling 2021 season. Valdez authored another this year. No major league pitcher has ever matched the single-season streak of 25 consecutive quality starts he produced in 2022. He handled business in both the American League Division Series and Championship Series. A final step remained.

Houston turned to him for World Series Game 2 seeking stability, something Valdez himself has sought for so long. All momentum left Minute Maid Park after Friday's five-run collapse in Game 1. Valdez recaptured it Saturday with a rousing start that spearheaded the Astros' 5-2 victory over the Philadelphia Phillies.

"The first inning is going to be the most intense moment," Nuñez told Valdez Saturday morning. "After this moment, you will get into the zone; your confidence will increase more and more.

"And after that, nobody can touch you."

Valdez tossed 22 pitches to procure those first three outs. Rhys Hoskins worked a one-out walk before Game 1 hero J.T. Realmuto struck out. Bryce Harper then lined out to left-center field to strand the free pass. Valdez exited the mound and mixed up his mojo.

He discarded his cleats, glove and belt in hopes of battling inefficiency with superstition.

"I normally have different spikes when I warm up and the ones that I go (with) into the game. Today I decided to start the game with the ones I warmed up in," Valdez said. "I had a long inning there (in the first), and I was like, 'You know what? I'm going to change everything.' Those are just things that us Dominicans do."

Outfitted better, Valdez punished the Phillies across the next six frames, exorcising a final set of demons during this season of dominance. He scattered four hits, struck out nine and surrendered one run across 6 1/3 innings. He protected both a three-run and five-run advantage, accomplishing what teammate and future Hall of Famer Justin Verlander could not in Game 1.

"He's a dog out there," said closer Ryan Pressly, who procured the game's final three outs. "He loves the spotlight. He loves these kinds of moments. It's fun to watch him from where he started to where he is now. He's been pitching out of his mind, and it's a testament to the work he put into the offseason and how he's gone about his year and how he prepares himself."

In punking the Phillies, Valdez generated nine ground-ball outs (including two on double plays) and subsisted on soft contact.

OPPOSITE: The Astros had a Game 2 ace up their sleeve in lefthander Framber Valdez, who got 18 of his 19 outs from either strikeouts (nine) or ground balls (seven, including two that resulted in double plays). **BRETT COOMER/HOUSTON CHRONICLE**

RIGHT: His third World Series start was a charm for Framber Valdez, whose first victory in the Fall Classic gave him six career postseason wins, tying Hall of Famer Pedro Martinez for most by a Dominican. A week later, Valdez would earn a seventh. **BRETT COOMER/HOUSTON CHRONICLE**

Philadelphia averaged just a 92.4 mph exit velocity on the 12 balls it put in play against him. Statcast classifies anything struck 95 mph or harder as "hard-hit."

"Best I've ever seen him," Astros center fielder Chas McCormick said. "His sinker was moving all over the place. His curveball was super sharp. He was great, so calm out there. … He can throw it right down the middle and still (get) soft contact. It's incredible."

The ability has always been there. Harnessing it became Valdez and Nuñez's primary focus. Too often, Valdez allowed an awkward bounce or a blown call to crater his outings. Nuñez implores him to breathe when such chaos is commencing. Smiling helps Valdez to settle his racing mind, so Nuñez encourages that, too.

Maturity is mandatory to blend into Houston's clubhouse culture. Valdez still has some moments when it wavers, but balance is far more apparent now than ever. Marriage and two sons — Franmei and Frayker — have helped. Both boys ran to meet their beaming dad following Saturday's game. Valdez's father attended Saturday's game, too, and saw his son pitch in person for the first time.

"It means the world to me he's here," Valdez said.

Valdez threw only 22 pitches without lead. No team in World Series history ha ever begun a game with three consecutiv extra-base hits. The Astros accomplished i on four first-inning pitches.

Jose Altuve, Jeremy Peña and Yorda Alvarez delivered three straight double off Phillies starter Zack Wheeler to stak Valdez to a two-run lead, and Alvarez score to make it 3-0 when, with two outs, Hoskin couldn't reel in a low throw to first base fro shortstop Edmundo Sosa.

Alex Bregman struck a hanging slider fo a two-run homer off Wheeler in the fifth providing Valdez the same 5-0 advantag

LEFT: Framber Valdez acknowledges a rousing sustained ovation as he leaves Game 2 in the seventh inning. The Minute Maid Park crowd of 42,926 included Valdez's father, who for the first time attended one of his son's major league games. **BRETT COOMER/HOUSTON CHRONICLE**

Verlander could not protect Friday night.

Valdez stepped onto the mound for the sixth and put it in peril. Kyle Schwarber worked a walk, and Hoskins crushed a curveball for a single — just the second curveball Philadelphia put in play all game. The middle of Philadelphia's order loomed for a chance to author another comeback. Valdez stepped off the mound before it could. Catcher Martín Maldonado meandered out toward him.

"That mound visit was way better than I was expecting," Maldonado said. "I went to the mound, and he said, 'I'm OK. I'm going to make pitches.' That's a huge step for him."

Realmuto readied himself while the conversation ceased. He saw five pitches before punching out, chasing a sinker Valdez elevated at 96.1 mph — more than 3 miles per hour above his season average.

Realmuto returned to the dugout, leaving just the reigning National League MVP between Valdez and a vintage escape. Harper was one of just two lefties in Philadelphia's lineup Saturday. Valdez is a ground ball generator. He supplied Harper a sinker down in the strike zone and received one.

The baseball bounced toward Altuve at second base. Valdez raced toward first in case of disaster. Altuve fed to Peña, whose relay to first baseman Yuli Gurriel beat Harper by three steps. Valdez pumped his fists and pointed toward his middle infield. A smile snuck across his face.

"A lot of it deals with concentration, just all the techniques I've learned to be able to calm myself down in those situations that are pressure-filled," Valdez said.

The man who taught it all sat in section 134, amid a crowd of 42,926 that rose to a sustained roar when Valdez exited the game during the seventh.

"I work with many pitchers on this team and watch them on TV," wrote Nuñez via text. "But some moments like this, they need you near."

WORLD
SERIES
27

Triple doubles

Led by a resurgent Jose Altuve, Astros get off to a bang-bang-bang start

BY DANIELLE LERNER · OCT. 29, 2022

A Phillies ace boasting a .118 opponents' batting average, 1.78 ERA and 0.51 WHIP in his first four postseason starts took the mound in Game 2 of the World Series at Minute Maid Park. The Astros decimated him with an ambush led by two men who, until Saturday, had fallen short of their offensive standard.

The first swing from Houston's slumping second baseman produced an unmistakably familiar sound and sight. Jose Altuve pounced on Zack Wheeler's initial offering and smacked a first-pitch double with a 103.8 mph exit velocity to the left-field warning track, igniting a long-dormant geyser. Minute Maid Park spewed applause. Old faithful was back.

Altuve and Yordan Alvarez were the only Astros starters to finish the regular season batting at least .300. As the team's No. 1 and No. 3 hitters, they are relied on to catalyze Houston's offense, but they entered Saturday a combined 11-for-70 (.157) in the playoffs with eight walks and 22 strikeouts in 80 plate appearances. In the Astros' 5-2 Game 2 win, they got on base six times and scored three runs.

Altuve's struggles stood in particularly stark contrast to his previous playoff history and the Astros' 7-1 start to the postseason. Manager Dusty Baker steadfastly pledged confidence in his leadoff man.

"You know just how I feel about Altuve. His track record speaks for itself," Baker said after Saturday's game. "I mean, he swung the bat great today. It was a good feeling to get him to lead off like he's been doing all year in the first inning. Boy, it was great to see. Hopefully, he can continue and start to roll the way Altuve can roll."

Altuve hit .368 (39-for-106) when swinging at the first pitch during the regular season. Before Saturday, he was 0-for-10 in the playoffs when doing so. He altered his luck within seconds and opened the floodgates for his team. The first three Astros batters of the game – Altuve, Jeremy Peña and Alvarez – all doubled.

"This guy right here set the tone, and it was awesome," Alex Bregman said, motioning to Altuve, who was seated to his right at a postgame interview table. "I feel like that one swing of the bat to start off the game got the crowd into it, got our dugout into it, got our offense going. We knew we were facing one of the best pitchers in the world today, and we just wanted to continue to try and battle and put together good at-bats."

Altuve's first-inning missile signaled a clear plan of attack against Wheeler. The Astros were aggressive and blitzed him early in at-bats, denying the righthander the ability to find comfort with any of the five pitches in his arsenal. They swung at his first five pitches and seven of the first nine.

"We all know he's a really good pitcher, but we also know his plan of attack was to attack hitters early in the count," Alvarez said through an interpreter. "And that's why we changed it, became aggressive, attacked him."

Wheeler threw 19 pitches in the first inning. Houston's hitters whiffed just twice and made contact on every swing they took on pitches in the zone, ending the inning with a 3-0 lead.

Peña replicated Altuve's line-drive double almost exactly, allowing the leadoff man to speed home and put Houston on the board. Alvarez yanked another RBI double off the left-field wall, then made a somewhat ambitious call to tag up on a fly ball and get to third. He scored when Phillies shortstop Edmundo Sosa made a two-out throwing error on a ground ball by Yuli Gurriel.

The Astros became the first team to start a World Series game with three consecutive extra-base hits. What's more, they proved it's much easier to win when your two best hitters are hitting.

After going 4-for-37 in his first eight playoff games, Altuve went 3-for-4 against the Phillies in Game 2. Alvarez went 1-for-3 with an RBI after he'd hit just .120 in his last 31 plate appearances following his incredible first two games of the AL Division Series.

"Yeah, we spoke about it, but you know, that's baseball," Alvarez said. "There are some highs. There are some lows. The important thing is we won those series. Happy to be here to contribute now."

OPPOSITE: After entering Game 2 hitting .108 (4-for-37) for the postseason, Jose Altuve got the stroke of luck (skill, actually) he was seeking. On the three occasions he led off an inning, Altuve doubled and scored in the first, singled in the fifth, and singled in the seventh, collecting three of the Astros' seven hits. KAREN WARREN/HOUSTON CHRONICLE

RIGHT: Yordan Alvarez doubles the pleasure of the Minute Maid Park faithful, putting the Astros up 2-0 in the bottom of the first with their third consecutive two-bagger against Zack Wheeler. **JON SHAPLEY/HOUSTON CHRONICLE**

Altuve said that after he started the postseason in an 0-for-25 funk, he spent more time in the cage and watching film of his at-bats, trying to pinpoint a problem. Eventually, he came to believe he was overloading his brain.

"I think that lately, the less I get on my mind, it's going to be better," he said. "So just try to simplify everything. Go out there, like Alex said, look for one pitch and put a good swing on the ball. That's what I did the last few days, and it's been working for me, and I've been feeling way better."

On Saturday, Altuve and Alvarez exemplified the threat Houston's offense poses when it executes a plan.

Wheeler averages 96 mph with both his four-seam fastball and his sinker and is known as a strike thrower. The Astros turned the tables on him and lit the righthander up for five runs (four earned) on six hits. They walked three times and struck out three times in his five innings.

Wheeler faced 24 batters, throwing 41 o his 69 pitches for strikes. Only twice did th Astros exceed five pitches in a plate appear ance against him.

"We're a pretty aggressive team, so I thin that just plays well for us," Astros cente fielder Chas McCormick said. "We like t swing the bat. He was in the zone, like h always is. He has a good slider, good cutte but everything is hard. We can hit hard.

LEFT: Still carrying a big stick, Alex Bregman hit his third home run of the playoffs. His two-run shot off Zack Wheeler in the fifth put the Astros up 5-0 and gave him nine RBIs in nine postseason games. **KAREN WARREN/HOUSTON CHRONICLE**

'as good to get a jump-start off him."

McCormick deserves credit for his two-ut single in the fourth inning, which, even fter Martín Maldonado lined out, allowed ne top of the Astros' order to lead off the fth inning.

With Houston up 3-0 and Wheeler still itching, Altuve sent a second-pitch curve-all up the middle for a single. After Peña ruck out, Alvarez grounded into a force ut at second base but sprinted down the first-base line to beat Sosa's throw and keep the inning alive.

Alvarez's hustle allowed Bregman to demolish a two-run homer, mirroring a sequence from ALCS Game 2 against the Yankees in which Alvarez set up a Bregman homer by beating a throw to first.

"I think the credit for that should go to Yordan for hustling down the line and keeping that inning alive, to be honest," Bregman said. "It was a bang-bang play at first. I feel like this team plays hard and never takes a pitch off. To be able to add some insurance was huge. … In all honesty, this is probably the most fun I ever had playing baseball."

Asked whether he believes opponents underestimate his speed, Alvarez smiled.

"I don't know. But hopefully, they continue to sleep on me and continue to fall asleep on some of those plays," he said. "Those little details are the ones that sometimes make the difference."

HOUSTON
ASTROS

WORLD SERIES GAME 3 // PHILLIES 7, ASTROS 0

Ambushed

Lance McCullers Jr. becomes first pitcher to give up five home runs in a World Series game

BY MATT YOUNG AND GREG RAJAN · NOV. 1, 2022

PHILADELPHIA — After Bryce Harper had rounded the bases, shouting "This is my house!" into a Fox television camera as he made his way to home plate, he made sure to relay a message to his teammates.

"Bohmer! Bohmer!" Harper yelled from the home dugout at Citizens Bank Park, trying to get the attention of on-deck hitter Alec Bohm. When Bohm walked over and leaned across the railing, Harper cupped a hand to his mouth and yelled something into the third baseman's ear.

What was said will be the subject of debate for a while. What is known: Bohm — just like Harper — homered on a first-pitch breaking ball. Bohm's shot to lead off the bottom of the second was the second of five home runs surrendered by Lance McCullers Jr. in the Astros' 7-0 loss in Game 3 of the World Series on Tuesday night.

On the TV broadcast, Hall of Fame pitcher John Smoltz said he believed McCullers was tipping his pitches, basically the same as having a tell in poker. A difference in delivery can indicate to a batter what pitch is coming.

"This has nothing to do with tipping," countered McCullers, who, as he has most of this season, refused to throw his fastball against lefthanded hitters such as Harper. "Clearly, they had a good game plan against me, and they executed better than I did."

With Harper, Bohm, Brandon Marsh, Rhys Hoskins and Kyle Schwarber all taking McCullers deep, the Phillies tied a World Series record with their five homers. McCullers is the first pitcher to surrender that many in one Series game.

Astros manager Dusty Baker said he and his coaches didn't pick up on anything McCullers might be doing to give away his pitches, and catcher Martín Maldonado agreed.

"I think it's about execution. I feel like we didn't execute," Maldonado said. "Too much of the slider on the plate to Hoskins; sinker ran all the way back against Bohm; 2-0 slider (Marsh) hit for a home run; changeup over the plate on Schwarber. Those guys have proved in the playoffs they can slug, and it's our job to stop it."

Whatever Harper told Bohm in that brief moment likely will remain a secret, but Harper didn't deny he was trying to help his teammate with something he picked up on during his at-bat.

"I think any time you have information, you want to be able to give that to your teammates at any point," Harper said. "Throughout the whole season, we've done that."

Bohm stuck to one-word answers when questioned about his conversation with Harper.

What did did he tell you? "Nothing," a smiling Bohm replied.

Whatever he said, was it helpful? "Maybe."

McCullers wasn't concerned with Harper's sharing anything he might have observed.

"I think guys have conversations all the time before at-bats and before innings and things like that," the righthander said. "I'm not going to sit here and say anything like that. I got whupped. End of story."

For the Citizens Bank throng of 45,712 who had endured a 13-year wait since Philadelphia last hosted a World Series game in 2009 – including an extra day after Game 3 was rained out Monday night – Tuesday's first 20 minutes set an impactful tone as the Phillies improved to 6-0 at home this postseason.

"We've been telling each other we've got to do what we can to punch first, especially while we're at home," Hoskins said. "It gets the crowd involved."

If the pregame ceremony that included Philadelphia sports greats Mike Schmidt, Julius Erving, Bernie Parent and Brandon Graham throwing out first pitches to members of the Phillies' 2008 championship team

OPPOSITE: Unfortunately for Lance McCullers Jr., some things can't be unseen, in this case a fifth-inning home run by Philadelphia's Rhys Hoskins. McCullers, who surrendered only four regular-season home runs in 47 2/3 innings, also gave up Game 3 dingers to Bryce Harper, Alec Bohm, Brandon Marsh and Kyle Schwarber as the Phillies tied a World Series record with five long balls. **KAREN WARREN/HOUSTON CHRONICLE**

OPPOSITE: Bryce Harper ignited the Phillie faithful watching their first home World Series game since 2009 with a two-run first-inning homer on the first offering he saw from Lance McCullers Jr. On the previous pitch he'd seen at Citizens Bank Park, Harper hit a decisive two-run homer in Philadelphia's National League Championship Series clincher over the San Diego Padres. **JON SHAPLEY/HOUSTON CHRONICLE**

didn't have hometown fans stirred up, Nick Castellanos definitely did.

Leading off the game, Jose Altuve lined Ranger Suárez's first-pitch sinker to short right field. The sinking line drive had an expected batting average of .560, but Castellanos, hardly known for his defensive prowess, made a sliding catch. It wasn't too different from his ninth-inning snag that denied the Astros a walk-off win in the series opener.

"That was an incredible play to start the game," Suárez said. "And it actually made me think, 'If we start like this, then we're only going to finish even better.' "

Suárez then retired Jeremy Peña on one pitch and struck out Yordan Alvarez to end a nine-pitch first inning. By evening's end, the lefthander became the second Venezuelan pitcher to earn a World Series win. The first, Freddy Garcia, earned his for the White Sox against the Astros in 2005.

On Oct. 4, the night after the Phillies had been up late celebrating a Minute Maid Park win that clinched their wild card berth, the Astros lit up Suárez for six runs on seven hits in three innings. On Tuesday, he allowed three hits and one walk in his five scoreless innings, striking out four.

The Phillies didn't take long to give Suárez all the runs he'd need. In the bottom of the first, Schwarber worked a six-pitch walk off McCullers. Two outs later, Harper crushed the second homer on the last two pitches he'd seen at home. His eighth-inning home run in Game 5 of the National League Championship Series against San Diego sent Philadelphia to the World Series. Tuesday's homer was also the sixth of this postseason for the NL's 2015 and 2021 Most Valuable Player.

"I'm running out of stuff to say about (Harper)," said Hoskins, whose homer also gave him six in this year's 14 playoff games for the Phils. "He's the most talented player I've ever played with. He's so in tune to the game and what's going on. It makes him so prepared in the box. ... We're used to seeing him be the guy, but it's cool to see him be the guy on baseball's biggest stage."

The way the Astros hit on that stage Tuesday, Harper's home run by itself was more than enough for the Phillies.

Houston totaled five hits against Suárez and relievers Connor Brogdon, Kyle Gibson, Nick Nelson and Andrew Bellatti. Batting second, Peña went 1-for-3 with a walk and was the only Astro to reach base with less than two outs. The other four men in the top five spots of the batting order — Altuve, Alex Bregman, Alvarez and Kyle Tucker — combined to go 0-for-15.

"I think today wasn't, obviously, a great day for our offense," Alvarez said through an interpreter. "We didn't get many guys on base, but then again, we also need to give their pitching staff a lot of credit."

Suárez's biggest out came when it was still a 2-0 game in the second. After Yuli Gurriel and designated hitter David Hensley (a rookie making his first postseason start) put runners at the corners with a pair of two-out singles, Suárez struck out Chas McCormick to end what would be the Astros' best threat of the night.

With a lead that reached 7-0 by the fifth, Phillies manager Rob Thomson could save his three best relievers — Zach Eflin, Seranthony Dominguez and Jose Alvarado — for later in the series and instead send out four less formidable arms.

During the second half of the season, Brogdon had a 4.26 ERA in 15 1/3 innings. Gibson had pitched just 1 1/3 innings in the last 30 days. Nelson had not pitched this postseason. Bellatti, typically a middle reliever, closed out a playoff game for the first time with a 1-2-3 ninth inning.

Asked whether their deficit sapped momentum from Astros hitters, Alvarez said it didn't factor in until the game was already out of hand.

"Early in the game, not really," he said. "We've fallen behind in the past, and we've come back from there, so we're used to doing that. Obviously, a lot later in the game, it gets a little bit more difficult to do when we haven't scored any runs and we're getting beat by a lot."

With the series far from decided, Baker said the Astros would go back to the drawing board.

"Sometimes they just hit you. You know what I mean?" the manager said. "It's pretty evident what kind of threat they pose. So we'll go back, and we'll figure it out."

Danielle Lerner contributed to this story.

Citizens Bank Park
s.com
phillies.com
WORLD SERIES
FTX

WORLD SERIES

WORLD SERIES GAME 4 // ASTROS 5, PHILLIES 0

The equalizer

Cristian Javier throws first six innings of second no-hitter in World Series history

BY BRIAN T. SMITH · NOV. 2, 2022

PHILADELPHIA — For Cristian Javier, it was the greatest gift he could give his parents.

Silencing the Phillies.

Handing the Astros a 5-0 victory in Game 4 of the World Series on Wednesday and ensuring the 2022 Fall Classic will return to Houston.

Throwing six innings of brilliant fire that became just the second no-hitter in World Series history.

"My dad arrived (Tuesday) to the United States, and (Wednesday) was the first time he saw me pitch," said Javier, through an interpreter.

A row of zeros filled Philadelphia's portion of the Jumbotron inside Citizens Bank Park as the Astros tied a back-and-forth Fall Classic at 2-2.

Javier for six frames. Then Bryan Abreu, Rafael Montero and Ryan Pressly for the final three as the 2022 Astros were forever linked with Don Larsen's perfect game for the New York Yankees in 1956.

This was a combined no-hitter for Dusty Baker's Astros, but it was just as perfect — especially after the Phillies blasted five home runs in the previous game.

"We've not finished the job yet, but this is very, very special for us," catcher Christian Vázquez said. "When we get old, we're going to remember this."

In his last six starts dating to Sept. 14, Javier has not allowed a run. Including an ALDS relief appearance against the Mariners in which he gave up a solo homer, the righthander known for his "invisiball" has allowed a ridiculous eight hits in his last 35 2/3 innings.

Javier should have started Game 3. That fact is obvious now. But he was the Astros' answer in Game 4, and No. 53 in bright orange was untouchable.

After all the zeros were frozen on the board, Javier revealed that his parents predicted he would throw a no-hitter.

"When they told me that, obviously, I got a lot more motivated," he said. "I kept my faith in God, and obviously, I knew I had a big commitment (Wednesday), being down 2-1 in the series. With my parents being here, I just tried to give my best, give my family the best that I could."

Javier was as smooth and calm as fire can be in the World Series.

Another burning fastball, perfectly placed at the bottom-right corner of the strike zone, smacked into Vázquez's waiting mitt.

Javier slowly circled the mound, then returned to the peak to dominate Philadelphia again.

The 25-year-old righthander, acquired as a $10,000 international signee from the Dominican Republic, struck out nine and allowed two walks while throwing 97 pitches, the same number Larsen threw when he beat the Dodgers 2-0 in Game 5 of the 1956 Series. Javier also moved the 106-win Astros within two victories of their second world championship.

How perfect was Game 4 for the Astros?

When Abreu took over in the bottom of the seventh to keep the no-hitter going, Bruce Springsteen was shown on the big screen. It was still 5-0 Astros, and the road team was making more beautiful noise than The Boss.

It was also Javier's second combined no-hitter in 2022. The third-year major leaguer helped shut down New York at Yankee Stadium on June 25.

"Very happy and very grateful to God for giving me this opportunity," Javier said. "I really didn't focus on the signing bonus. I just tried to do the best that I could every single year. And I knew every single year that I was in the minors that I didn't have anything promised, that I would just have to give my best every single year out. And thankfully, I'm here."

Paired with Vázquez, Javier owned Philly. He sucked out the stadium's once-swirling pride and reminded baseball devotees across

OPPOSITE: A strikeout to end the first was merely a sign of things to come for Cristian Javier, who put his name in baseball's history books by throwing six innings in the first combined no-hitter in MLB postseason history. Javier was the 10th pitcher in World Series annals to no-hit an opponent through six innings and only the third since Don Larsen's perfect game for the Yankees in 1956. Coincidentally, the 97 pitches thrown by Javier in six innings matched Larsen's total for nine. **KAREN WARREN/HOUSTON CHRONICLE**

the world how much power a single starting arm can still hold in the Fall Classic.

The Astros lost Game 3 in a 7-0 blowout, setting up a near must-win on Wednesday.

Javier blended fastballs with sliders, constantly painting the edges of the zone and erasing bat after bat with modern mound artistry.

"It's crazy," said Alex Bregman, whose two-run double in a five-run fifth inning gave the Astros a 3-0 lead, one batter after Yordan Alvarez was hit by a pitch with the bases loaded. "We grew up watching the World Series. We know that baseball's been going on for a long, long time. So to be a part of — just be a teammate on a team that did that and what Javy and all the guys did — is really special. It's a moment that we'll all cherish forever and we'll all remember forever. It was really awesome."

Javier struck out J.T. Realmuto, Bryce Harper and Nick Castellanos in the fourth as the core of the Phillies' lineup failed to connect with put-away fastballs that ranged between 93 and 95 mph.

The Astros, who had gone 16 innings without scoring, finally backed their pitcher in a game-changing fifth. It was 1-0 Astros, then 3-0 Astros. It was 4-0 on Kyle Tucker's sacrifice fly and 5-0 on Yuli Gurriel's RBI single as the road team kept piling on in Game 4.

The flip side of the Astros' sudden barrage: Javier would return to the mound whenever his club finished attacking at the plate.

Alec Bohm struck out to begin the Philadelphia fifth. Bryson Stott did the same. Jean Segura popped out. Another inning for Javier as he kept throwing speedballs by the whiffing Phillies.

Brandon Marsh grounded out. Kyle Schwarber did the same. Rhys Hoskins also hit into nothingness.

Six innings of futility for Philadelphia.

Six no-hit frames for Javier, who just kept firing and firing in the silenced Philly night.

His right arm ensured that the World Series will return to Minute Maid Park on Saturday.

"It was the best gift that I could have ever given (my parents)," Javier said. "I know that they're really proud of me for what I was able to accomplish."

RIGHT: Yordan Alvarez breaks up a scoreless game the hard way in the top of the fifth, getting hit with the bases loaded on the first pitch thrown by Phillies reliever Jose Alvarado. Alvarado had just entered after the Astros chased starter Aaron Nola with singles by Chas McCormick, Jose Altuve and Jeremy Peña to begin the inning. **KAREN WARREN/HOUSTON CHRONICLE**

OPPOSITE: Alex Bregman continues Houston's fifth-inning outburst with a two-run double off Jose Alvarado to make it 3-0. The lead grew to 5-0 on Kyle Tucker's sacrifice fly and Yuli Gurriel's RBI single as the Astros batted around. **BRETT COOMER/HOUSTON CHRONICLE**

WORLD SERIES
EASTON

WORLD SERIES
ASTROS
52

Easy as 7-8-9

Bryan Abreu, Rafael Montero, Ryan Pressly add three-inning coda to no-hit parade

BY STEVE SCHAEFFER · NOV. 2, 2022

PHILADELPHIA – Finishing no-hitters started by Cristian Javier is becoming old hat for Ryan Pressly. In Game 4 of the World Series, Bryan Abreu and Rafael Montero also got a piece of history.

Once Javier was removed after six innings and 97 pitches Wednesday night at Citizens Bank Park, Abreu, Montero and Pressly finished only the second no-hitter in 118 Fall Classics, a 5-0 gem over the Phillies that evened this year's Series at two games apiece.

Don Larsen's 1956 perfect game for the Yankees against the Dodgers was the first Series no-no, back in the day when removing a starting pitcher from such a game was unthinkable. The only other postseason no-hitter was Roy Halladay's complete effort for the Phillies against the Reds in a 2010 National League Division Series opener.

But this is baseball 2022. And with the Astros in position to hand Philadelphia its first loss in seven home games this postseason, manager Dusty Baker didn't hesitate to turn to his relievers.

"We had a real fresh bullpen, one of the best bullpens around," said Baker, coincidentally the opposing skipper in Halladay's gem. "So I had full faith that they could do the job."

Abreu's seventh inning was practically a carbon copy of Javier's fourth. Facing the heart of Philadelphia's lineup, Abreu struck out J.T. Realmuto, Bryce Harper and Nick Castellanos swinging.

"I've been watching Javier from the bullpen, and he was using his fastball," Abreu said. "And I just have to come in and throw my fastball, too."

But while Javier put away the Phillies' 3-4-5 hitters exclusively with fastballs, Abreu used his heater to set up Realmuto and Castellanos with third-strike sliders. The 25-year-old Dominican didn't shy away from Harper, however, retiring the two-time MVP with his hardest pitch of the inning, a 99.7 mph four-seamer.

Montero entered in the eighth and fanned the first hitter he faced, Alec Bohm, then retired Bryson Stott on a fly to left. Perhaps Philadelphia's best chance all night at a hit on a fair ball came when Jean Segura lined sharply to right field. But newly minted Gold Glover Kyle Tucker corralled the ball rather easily, keeping the no-hitter intact.

Pressly took the mound in the ninth. On June 25, he finished a three-pitcher no-hitter at Yankee Stadium in which Javier lasted seven innings. Héctor Neris was the eighth-inning bridge on that Saturday afternoon. Did Pressly think he'd be finishing another no-no started by Javier?

"In the World Series? No," Pressly said. "You don't really think about that coming into the World Series. For it to happen tonight and be a part of it, it's something special."

Pressly struck out Brandon Marsh before walking Kyle Schwarber, who rifled two foul balls to the right side during his at-bat. In an earlier plate appearance against Javier, Schwarber drilled a ball that just missed going fair over the first-base bag, the closest thing the Phillies had to a hit in the game.

When the count reached 3-2 on Schwarber, Pressly said he wasn't necessarily thinking about not giving in.

"Schwarber's a great hitter through and through," Pressly said. "You want to be careful with him, but at the same time, you've got a pretty decent lead, so you just want to attack hitters at that point."

After Schwarber's walk, Pressly retired Rhys Hoskins on a fly to Tucker before Alex Bregman deftly fielded a hard-hit one-hopper to third and easily threw out Realmuto to preserve the first combined no-hitter in MLB postseason history.

"Once I saw Breggy scoop it, I already knew it was over," said Pressly, who in eight postseason appearances this year has a 0.00 ERA and 0.72 WHIP. "If it's a bad throw over there or anything, Yuli (Gurriel) is probably one of the best at picking it. So as soon as that ground ball hit Breggy's glove, I was pretty comfortable."

In Pressly's mind, the most important thing about the Astros' Game 4 victory was rebounding from their 7-0 loss in Game 3 and evening a series now guaranteed to

OPPOSITE: Astros reliever Bryan Abreu kept the Game 4 no-hitter intact with 1-2-3 seventh in which struck out J.T. Realmuto, Bryce Harper and Nick Castellanos, all swinging. KAREN WARREN/HOUSTON CHRONICLE

STROS
47

return to Houston.

"You get slapped in the face yesterday, and you want to come back today and make a statement," Pressly said. "You try to have the mind of a goldfish in this game. You try not to think about anything. You just want to go out there and produce and put a W in the column."

OPPOSITE: Rafael Montero made quick work of the Phillies in the eighth, striking out Alec Bohm before retiring Bryson Stott on a fly to left and Jean Segura on a liner to right. **KAREN WARREN/HOUSTON CHRONICLE**

LEFT: Working around a one-out walk to Kyle Schwarber in the ninth, Astros closer Ryan Pressly finished the second no-hitter in World Series history and the third in MLB postseason annals. **BRETT COOMER/HOUSTON CHRONICLE**

WORLD SERIES
HOUSTON ASTROS
THERMA-FIT
THERMA-FIT

LEFT: There's a line at Citizens Bank, with J.J. Matijevic, from left, Korey Lee (both on the Astros' World Series taxi squad), Bryan Abreu, Yordan Alvarez and Christian Javier eager to congratulate Ryan Pressly for closing out the Astros' second combined no-hitter of 2022. BRETT COOMER/HOUSTON CHRONICLE

ABOVE: All told, there were five men with a hand in the Astros' Game 4 no-hitter: Rafael Montero, from left, Bryan Abreu, Cristian Javier, catcher Christian Vázquez, and Ryan Pressly. KAREN WARREN/HOUSTON CHRONICLE

WORLD SERIES
WORLD SERIES

WORLD SERIES GAME 5 // ASTROS 3, PHILLIES 2

High drama

Pins-and-needles thriller puts Astros on precipice of title, nets Justin Verlander first World Series win

BY CHANDLER ROME · NOV. 3, 2022

PHILADELPHIA — An epic ended in the shower, soaking the shirt of a 39-year-old ace acting half his age. He received treatment reserved for rookies who reach their first major league milestones. They're thrown into a laundry cart, rolled into a shower and sprayed with everything a clubhouse cafeteria has to offer. One whiff of Justin Verlander made it apparent alcohol was involved.

Two years away left Verlander with a renewed perspective and more appreciation for the sport he makes seem simple. He spends more time in the clubhouse and makes a concerted effort to counsel young players who need it. Teammates have noticed a newer version of an ace who always seemed austere and sometimes unapproachable. Thursday turned him back into a 23-year-old without a care or concern in the world, a man willing to share his joy with so many around him.

"It's so symbolic that so many people were a part of this win," Verlander said, a wide smile affixed to his face. "They rallied around me, and they were almost just as happy that I got the win as I was."

None of the nine victories preceding this one in the Astros' postseason produced more heroes or generated more heartburn than Thursday's 3-2 win at Citizens Bank Park. Houston's list of legendary Game 5 escapes now has a new addition. None can top the 25-run, 10-frame win over the Dodgers from five seasons ago, but both put the Astros in the same scenario: one win away from a World Series title.

"Little stressful," Kyle Tucker deadpanned, "but it's all right."

Modesty is Tucker's trademark. What transpired Thursday night in south Philadelphia illustrates this team's identity better than any of the 173 contests that came before it. A club predicated on pitching and preventing runs prevailed playing the sort of game it is conditioned to win.

"(We continued) to do what got us here," Verlander said after earning his first win in a World Series. "What makes this team so great is there's not one particular person that's going to try to go out there and try to be the hero on any given night. We just try to have quality at-bats, try to make quality pitches, try to go to our bullpen with a lead."

Verlander's World Series failures are almost inexplicable. The same right arm, repertoire and reputation that arrive every April appear in October. Wear from a six-month regular season weakens everyone in this sport, but Verlander's career is defined by defying such convention and succeeding when others would wither.

He's excelled everywhere but here, the one place where baseball's best cement their legacies. Across eight starts in five separate World Series, Verlander vacillated from vintage to vulnerable, an abrupt about-face that forced four separate managers to make uncomfortable choices. His pregame meeting with catcher Martín Maldonado featured a simple message.

"Give us everything you got," Maldonado said he told him. "We got an off day tomorrow. Our bullpen is really good. Don't try to do too much. Just execute pitches."

Before the game, manager Dusty Baker proclaimed Verlander had "no leash." Trust is fine. Too much of it in the postseason can torpedo a team's chances. Games 1 and 3 of the World Series demonstrated it. More blame belongs with Verlander and Lance McCullers Jr. for their poor execution, but the bench's blind faith in both men to turn around their outings only put the Astros in a bigger predicament.

Verlander took the mound Thursday and, early on, looked nothing like his regular-season self. Kyle Schwarber swatted the second pitch he threw into the right-field seats. Philadelphia had a clear plan to ambush his fastball and force Verlander to spin more

OPPOSITE: Having surrendered a two-out double to Bryce Harper, Justin Verlander was pumped after retiring Nick Castellanos to end the fifth inning and preserve a 2-1 Astros lead. During his 10-pitch at-bat, Castellanos fouled off three 2-2 pitches and one 3-2 pitch before flying to left. The out put Verlander in position for his first World Series victory, and Houston's bullpen did the rest from there. KAREN WARREN/HOUSTON CHRONICLE

RIGHT: Continuing his pointed response to any who doubted him after a rough postseason start, Jose Altuve stands at third after leading off Game 5 with a double and advancing an extra base on an error by Phillies center fielder Brandon Marsh. Altuve would score the first run on Jeremy Peña's RBI single. **KAREN WARREN/HOUSTON CHRONICLE**

sliders. Early on, he could not, creating many of the situations Baker trusts him to escape.

Baker and pitching coach Josh Miller unleashed a modern clinic in game management when they arose. They managed Game 5 with more urgency than at any previous point in this postseason. Ryne Stanek started to throw after two batters reached against Verlander during the second. Bryan Abreu warmed before the fourth inning even began. Héctor Neris did so prior to the fifth.

"I remember my teammate Tommy John always told me that a good pitcher can get out of trouble twice, a great pitcher three times, and a so-so pitcher maybe one time," Baker said "I could hear Tommy John talking to me during the game. Sometimes you call upon people that you've played with or talked to in the past to deal with the present."

Seven of Philadelphia's first 16 hitters reached against Verlander. Four Phillies struck balls 95 mph or harder. By the third inning, he ended a streak of 55 consecutiv starts with fewer than four walks. He walke four batters total in August. On Thursday four of the first 13 Phillies he faced got fre passes.

Schwarber struck Verlander's second pitc 368 feet to the right-field seats. The four-seam fastball arrived at 93.2 mph, almost tw miles per hour below Verlander's season average. No pitcher has permitted more Worl Series home runs than the 10 Verlander now

LEFT: After crossing paths with Phillies catcher J.T. Realmuto on a fourth-inning homer that put the Astros up 2-1, Jeremy Peña flashes the heart sign that became a notable element of his prodigious postseason. The sign, Peña said, was dedicated to his mother. **KAREN WARREN/HOUSTON CHRONICLE**

has. Schwarber's blast sent him past Catfish Hunter for the dubious distinction.

"Those guys out there are tough outs," Maldonado said. "They were ambushing the fastball, and he didn't settle in until the third or fourth inning."

Verlander's slider started to return to its most menacing form. Velocity on his fastball reached its season average instead of a tick below. He struck out four straight batters between the fourth and fifth before Bryce Harper hammered a two-out double into the right-field corner. With the Astros up 2-1, Neris continued to warm.

Baker stuck with his ace. Up came Nick Castellanos, Verlander's teammate for parts of five seasons with the Detroit Tigers. The two men know each other's tendencies. Verlander threw everything at his disposal.

Castellanos saw 10 pitches in all — five sliders, two four-seamers, two curveballs and a seventh-pitch changeup. After Castellanos sent it foul, Maldonado jogged to the mound.

"He wanted one pitch; I wanted another one," Maldonado said. "Like I always do in those situations, I wanted to make sure we were on the same page. This time, I went to his pitch."

The crowd rose to a crescendo, creating the type of World Series tension Verlander has never conquered. He supplied two curveballs, the pitch he preferred to throw. Castellanos spoiled one foul and laid off another.

RIGHT: Trying to score on a grounder to third base, the Astros' Yuli Gurriel got caught in a seventh-inning rundown in which he collided with Phillies first baseman Rhys Hoskins, who applied the tag on a 5-2-6-3 play. Gurriel took the field in the bottom of the inning but was lifted for pinch hitter Trey Mancini in the eighth because of knee soreness. Gurriel missed the rest of the World Series with a sprain of his right MCL. **KAREN WARREN/HOUSTON CHRONICLE**

Verlander reached back for his best pitch, the one carrying him through this trudge of a start. In Game 1, Castellanos hooked a slider for a single into shallow left field.

This one darted down and away and generated a swing. The baseball traveled 298 feet toward Yordan Alvarez in left field. Verlander tracked its flight and left the mound once he realized the result. He pounded his glove and offered a yell. The leash he lengthened had reached its end.

"That's why that guy is one of the best," Maldonado said. "He's never satisfied. He's always going to get better. He was a little bit out of rhythm the first couple innings. Sat down for quite a while in the first inning, but he kept us in the ballgame. That's all we could ask."

After tallying two runs against Phillies opener Noah Syndergaard on Jeremy Peña's first-inning RBI single and fourth-innin homer, the Astros conducted a clinic i squandering scoring chances. They strande seven baserunners and finished 1-for-11 wit men in scoring position.

Yuli Gurriel started the seventh with double and went to third on a wild pitch then broke home on Chas McCormick's one out ground ball to third base. Philadelphi executed a rundown and injured Gurriel i

LEFT: On a perfectly executed hit-and-run play in the eighth, Jose Altuve slides into second on his way to third as a ball hit by Jeremy Peña finds a hole just behind him. Altuve would score a huge insurance run for the Astros on Yordan Alvarez's grounder to first base. KAREN WARREN/HOUSTON CHRONICLE

he process of tagging him out. His right knee collided with fellow first baseman Rhys Hoskins.

The Astros made it 3-1 in the eighth on Alvarez's grounder to first scoring Altuve, who'd gone to third on a perfectly executed hit-and-run single by Peña. But Trey Mancini, pinch-hitting for Gurriel, stranded two more runners with a strikeout that left him hitless in 18 postseason at-bats.

Mancini then entered for his first defensive inning of the postseason. He said he had not taken ground balls at first base since a nondescript workout day sometime in October.

"I thought there was a much better chance of me going into the outfield at some point first," Mancini said. "I've been trying to focus my time there."

First base needed him now, in the eighth inning of a two-run game Rafael Montero made a mess of. Montero faced four batters. Three reached. Nine of his 17 pitches missed the strike zone, four apiece to Castellanos and Bryson Stott, putting Montero in a hellish predicament. Jean Segura struck an 0-1 fastball into right field, chasing Castellanos home and trimming Houston's lead to one. Baker called on his closer to protect it and procure the final five outs.

A strikeout of Brandon Marsh gave Ryan

RIGHT: Greatest catch in Astros history? Center fielder Chas McCormick might lay claim to it after robbing Philadelphia's J.T. Realmuto of extra bases for the second out of the ninth and Houston clinging to a 3-2 lead. KAREN WARREN/HOUSTON CHRONICLE

Pressly the first. He stood a strike away from a second against Schwarber. The slider he spun sat a tad up. Schwarber whacked it down the first-base line. Mancini leaned to his left and snagged the shot Statcast assigned a .560 expected batting average.

"I'm glad the ball was fair and he didn't get another shot to swing," Baker said.

The alternative did not afford much more comfort. Pressly's ninth included Hoskins, J.T. Realmuto and Harper — the most potent part of Philadelphia's lineup. Hoskins struck out before Realmuto ripped a hanging slider into the gap in right-center field.

McCormick and Tucker converged on the baseball. McCormick's mere presence was a surprise. Baker often likes to put Mauricio Dubón in center field late in close games and shift McCormick to left. Holding just a one-run lead, Baker opted to keep Alvarez in left field so as not to take his bat out of the lineup in case the game went into extras.

Realmuto threatened to send it there. Hi missile traveled 387 feet. Off the bat, Tucke did not think McCormick had a chance.

"I didn't know how well he hit it, Maldonado said, "but I knew it was in th gap. As a team, we take a lot of pride in ou defense."

A run prevention team must have suc standards. McCormick leapt at the out-of town scoreboard and secured the baseball a the height of his leap. He fell toward the dir

LEFT: Manager Dusty Baker was exceedingly grateful to Ryan Pressly after the closer's five-out save gave the Astros a 3-2 Series edge over the Phillies. **BRETT COOMER/HOUSTON CHRONICLE**

and raised his glove. Tucker pumped his fists.

"It's a phenomenal catch," Tucker said. "Probably one of the best catches, just given the scenario and the difficulty of it."

Pressly plunked Harper with a breaking ball before Castellanos chopped the final out to shortstop. The sight sent Houston's dugout spilling onto the field. Hugs and handshakes were exchanged all around. A collective exhale could be heard from Houston, which can watch its club clinch a championship as early as Saturday.

"We're just trying to stay grounded," said Peña, whose home run was his fourth of the postseason. "We're going to just lock back in and play our game. Show up ready to go, ready to compete and try to close it out."

One task stood in the team's way. Verlander finished his on-field interviews and descended the steps into Houston's clubhouse. A crowd awaited him. Champagne and an empty laundry cart at the ready, his teammates razzed the ace who relied on them for a milestone.

"I can say I got one," Verlander said of his long-awaited World Series victory. "My boys, my teammates, my family, they gave me the rookie treatment after the game. They put me in the cart and rolled me in the shower and just doused me with all sorts of stuff, and it was one of the best feelings in my career. Just truly love these guys. I love our team."

WORLD SERIES
ASTROS
ASTROS
ASTROS
55
47

WORLD SERIES GAME 6 // ASTROS 4, PHILLIES 1

Indisputable champions

\stros answer three years of derision with their second crown

3Y CHANDLER ROME • NOV. 5, 2022

In the only ballpark where they're beloved and atop a sport they waited three seasons o silence, the greatest group of Astros ever ssembled gathered one final time. Kyle Tucker sprinted to his left, secured a sinking ine drive and sent bodies bounding from he first-base dugout. Delirium overtook the eam that cemented a dynasty.

A club composed of young and old, omegrown heroes and hired hands, natives f seven countries, and a manager whose aseball life spans seven decades coalesced nto something closer knit than anyone could athom. Derision only deepened their bond nd brought them together. Boos serenaded hem like a summer soundtrack. Winning n spite of them became the Astros' weekly radition.

Silencing an opposing stadium and enire sport shouldn't be so simple. This team urned it into standard operating procedure. t conquered all comers and calmed the caophony of visiting crowds, many booing a rand more than the ballplayers representing t. That "everyone against us" attitude emlazoned on T-shirts turned tangible inside he Astros' clubhouse, where 26 players and 1 coaches grew cognizant that all they had vere each other. They needed nothing more.

"These kids have gone through a lot," said ench coach Joe Espada. "And watching how they have matured and endured a lot of noise and criticism and stuff like that ... (I've watched) them push that away and say, 'You know what? We're a great team. We're going to play for one another, play for this city and represent people with respect.' And you know what? We did it."

Scandal threatened to implode an infrastructure shaped for sustained success. The team spent three seasons salvaging its reputation. Baseball's most respected manager arrived to mend wounds, work his magic, and win the one game missing from his Hall of Fame résumé. Players sought to prove talent, not trash cans, propelled them toward dynastic territory.

"We didn't need to do that. It proves that we're a good team no matter what," said outfielder Chas McCormick. "We've got great players on this team. With all the crap talked about 2017, I'm just happy that Houston got one in 2022. We deserve this one."

When the Astros obtained it, Houston hosted the sort of party this city has craved. No World Series winner in nine years had clinched the championship at home. At 10:17 p.m. Saturday, after three hours and 13 minutes and the type of game this team mastered, the Astros finished their only stated goal.

Their 4-1 win over the Philadelphia Phillies at Minute Maid Park secured the second World Series title in franchise history and first for Baker in his 25th managerial season. Coaches mobbed him in the first-base dugout after the final out while players piled onto the pitcher's mound.

"I always said before that if I win one, you know, I'll win two. But you've got to win one first," Baker said. "I mean, the one was hell to get to this point. But it was well worth it. I'm in a great city with great people, great fans, and I've got a great ballclub."

For five years, Houston sought a second World Series title. Speculation and shadiness still envelop the first. The legacy of the 2017 team — and the Astros' success since — felt incomplete without another championship. Winning another would be redemptive.

"Of course we did (need to win another one). It's pretty obvious," Astros owner Jim Crane said. "The team's been good, and it's hard to win these things. (In 2019) we had the best team on paper, and we didn't win."

Only that Houston club won more regular-season games (107) than this one (106). It ran roughshod through the American League playoffs only to wither against the Washington Nationals in a Game 7 loss that will linger for however long Houston plays baseball.

"On the other side of that," general manager James Click said, "I felt that was one

OPPOSITE: Pitchers and catchers reported, along with everyone else, to the Minute Maid Park infield once the Astros wrapped up the 2022 championship. JON SHAPLEY/HOUSTON CHRONICLE

RIGHT: Framber Valdez became a 20-game winner of sorts after allowing one run in six innings in Game 6. His three postseason victories followed 17 in the regular season. Valdez also joined Hall of Famer Sandy Koufax as the only lefthanders to strike out five consecutive batters in a World Series game. As part of a nine-K performance, the Astros southpaw fanned Kyle Schwarber, Rhys Hoskins and J.T. Realmuto in the fourth and Bryce Harper and Nick Castellanos in the fifth. **KAREN WARREN/HOUSTON CHRONICLE**

of the best baseball teams I've ever seen from top to bottom."

Four months later, Crane hired Click from the Tampa Bay Rays to shepherd his franchise through scandal. He paired the forward-thinking executive with Baker, a manager brought up in a bygone era. The odd couple had its clashes but thrice put Houston on the precipice of a championship.

Before trying again to secure it, Click considered the legacy at stake. A pregame talk with Espada on Saturday included discussions of that 2019 Houston club. Click reiterated it as the best he'd ever seen.

"(Esapada) looked at me, and he said, 'This team is better,'" Click said. "I think Joe is right."

Twenty-two pitchers used over the course of the season formed the most formidable staff in franchise history. Dominant defense buoyed it. Alex Bregman and Jose Altuve reprised their roles as superstars. Tucker and Yordan Alvarez ascended into that echelon. A rookie shortstop rose above expectations and excelled in place of a departed cornerstone. Jeremy Peña struck two more singles Saturday, finished the World Series 10-for-27, and earned Most Valuable Player honors.

The Astros matched a franchise recor with 117 total wins, executing a seven-mont mockery of the major leagues. Houston led th American League West for 125 consecutiv games to conclude the regular season. The Ne York Yankees finished seven games behind th Astros for AL supremacy. Houston swept the in four games to capture the pennant.

"No matter what happens, if we had the lead

LEFT: Third baseman Alex Bregman, whose three assists in Game 6 included one that started a first-inning double play, was errorless in the Astros' 13 postseason games. **KAREN WARREN/HOUSTON CHRONICLE**

ve kept the lead," Hall of Famer Jeff Bagwell said. "And even if the game was tied, we still won the game."

Leverage innings created this club's legacy. Finding one they didn't win is almost impossible. No team in baseball boasted a better bullpen. Few had a lineup with more postseason pedigree. Pairing the two produced a club incapable of coughing anything up. Houston's relievers surrendered six runs in 54 1/3 playoff innings. Its lineup never lit up scoreboards but still struck out just 118 times in 13 games, forcing flawless execution from opponents incapable of it.

"We're nasty. Our bullpen is nasty. It's unbelievable," said closer Ryan Pressly. "These guys go out there, throw, make quality pitches. That's what we do."

Pressly procured the final out of a game — and series — his club is conditioned to win. The Astros' pitching depth deadened Philadelphia's potent lineup for five of the six contests. A five-homer outburst in Game 3 became an outlier. The Phillies produced three runs across the final three games. Four Houston hurlers no-hit them in Game 4. Four held the Phillies to one run Saturday.

"In the end, I think we were able to show why we were the best team this season," ace Justin Verlander said. "You can pick a game. Tonight, it was the slugging and pitching."

Starter Framber Valdez mauled the Phillies for six spectacular innings. Philadelphia inflated his pitch count but inflicted little damage aside from Kyle Schwarber's sixth-inning solo home run. Valdez allowed four of the first eight

RIGHT: Kyle Schwarber, who led the National League with 46 home runs in the regular season for Philadelphia, broke a scoreless tie when he went deep against Astros starter Framber Valdez in the top of the sixth. It was Schwarber's sixth home run of the postseason. **KAREN WARREN/HOUSTON CHRONICLE**

men he faced to get aboard. Two worked walks, one took a breaking ball off the foot, and one singled. Valdez stranded three of them and erased the other by inducing a double play.

None of the next 10 Phillies reached. Valdez ran off five straight strikeouts in the third and fourth innings. He and Sandy Koufax are the only lefthanded pitchers to accomplish that in a World Series game.

For five innings, Houston offered Valdez no support. The lineup had no recourse for Philadelphia's Zack Wheeler, who wielded the same terrifying arsenal that produced a 2.82 regular-season ERA. His four-seam fastball reached 99.1 mph and averaged 98. His sinker sat at 97.2 mph.

Wheeler yielded 13 batted balls in play. None exited a Houston bat harder than 96 mph. He struck out Altuve twice and Bregman once. Two of the three punchouts arrived with men aboard. Altuve began the postseason 0-for-25 and finished it 11-for-58. The malaise would cripple other clubs.

Houston absorbed it much like everything else. Peña blossomed into a bona fide star. McCormick offered a boost from the bottom of the lineup. Yuli Gurriel found a fountain of youth until a knee sprain sent him to the bench for Game 6.

Saturday's lineup scuffled against Wheeler. It struck two singles across five innings. Wheeler started the sixth with a gift: light-hitting Martín Maldonado in the batter's box. The third pitch Wheeler threw struck Maldonado's elbow. The catcher walked to first base and turned the lineup over.

Altuve grounded a fielder's choice to third base. Peña willed a single through the middle, forcing Rob Thomson into a decision. With runners at the corners and Alvarez looming, the Phillies manager's best lefthanded relieve[r] stood ready in the bullpen. Thomson sum[-]moned him.

Two heroic home runs in the American Leagu[e] Division Series etched Alvarez into Astros play[-]off lore. He had done nearly nothing afterward[,] bringing a 5-for-40 slump into Saturday's game[.] Hitting coach Troy Snitker noticed him placin[g] no weight on his back foot in his batting stance[.] A correction happened during Game 4 but ha[d] yet to produce tangible results.

Two fly outs Saturday sent Alvarez searchin[g]

LEFT: Don't sleep on Game 6 designated hitter Christian Vázquez, who engaged in some pillow talk after delivering an RBI single that capped the Astros' four-run sixth. **KAREN WARREN/HOUSTON CHRONICLE**

or a breakthrough against José Alvarado. The tocky southpaw spins a menacing sinker. lvarez saw three of them. All exceeded 98 nph. The final 98.9 mph offering bisected ome plate. Alvarez dropped his barrel and nade contact.

"As soon as he hit the ball, I was like, 'Welp, 'm going to start getting ready,' " Pressly said.

The baseball flew to a place few reach. A rassy batter's eye at Minute Maid Park sits 0 feet off the ground in dead center field. lvarez's fly ball cleared it. Statcast measured he distance at 450 feet.

Those who say they saw it land will kid themselves. Why watch when fate is sealed? The swing sent a ballpark into bedlam and Houston's bullpen into action. A three-run advantage, created by Christian Vázquez's RBI single later in the sixth, felt like 20 for this pen.

The crowd came to a crescendo and started to count outs. Only the Los Angeles Dodgers won more regular-season games (111) than Houston. They did not survive their Division Series, a sobering reminder that baseball rarely rewards its best regular-season team. As the class of the American League, the 2022 Astros bucked the trend.

"Every single person contributed — from our bullpen to our starters to our bench guys, our minor league guys that came up," Bagwell said. "This team is just such a complete team. It's been amazing to watch."

Distancing Houston from its misdeeds is difficult. One step inside a visiting ballpark is proof, even if only five players from the 2017 club remain. The second championship team is a shell of the first.

Turnover that cripples other clubs does not change this one. Three consecutive American League Championship Series appearances after the sign-stealing revelations proved it. George Springer left following the first. Carlos Correa exited after the second.

Faces change, and the Astros still ascend. No franchise is functioning with such precision. Championship Series appearances have become birthrights. Pennants are purely decorative. The standard here is higher. Saturday, it was reached.

"It proves we're the best team in baseball for the past five, six years," Maldonado said. "They have nothing to say now."

RIGHT: Pitching against the Phillies was an emotional experience for Astros reliever Héctor Neris, whose clean seventh inning included strikeouts of former Philadelphia teammates Alec Bohm and Jean Segura. **KAREN WARREN/HOUSTON CHRONICLE**

OPPOSITE: Astros reliever Bryan Abreu concluded a remarkable postseason in which he threw 11 1/3 scoreless innings by striking out Kyle Schwarber to end the eighth. The Phillies slugger fanned 200 times during the regular season, but there was a surprising element to this K: With the count 1-and-2, Schwarber fouled off a bunt attempt. **KAREN WARREN/HOUSTON CHRONICLE**

STROS
BA
44

ASTROS
ASTROS.COM
FTX

No doubt about it

The best summation of Yordan Alvarez's 450-foot home run? 'You cannot hit the ball up there.'

BY DANIELLE LERNER · NOV. 5, 2022

Needing one more win to capture a second World Series title and absolve themselves from scorn and scandal, the Astros were scoreless and losing by a run going to the bottom of the sixth inning Saturday night. Redemption and the continuation of a dynasty, it seemed, would be delayed for at least another night.

Baseball players and coaches are fond of saying a slumping player is "due" for a hit. Astros manager Dusty Baker often cites the law of averages. Others predicate their belief on mechanical adjustments and matchups.

If you believe in faith and fate, as Yordan Alvarez does, equilibrium was restored during Game 6. One home run appeared to dent the Astros' championship hopes before another resuscitated them.

When Alvarez came up to bat in the sixth inning with the Phillies ahead 1-0, he had six hits in his last 54 plate appearances. Nevertheless, the events of the previous 24 hours had led him to be overcome by a sense of peace.

His daughter's fourth birthday is Sunday, and Alvarez's wife said the best gift would be a championship. On Friday's off day, the slugger received words of encouragement from various family members.

When Alvarez arrived at Minute Maid Park on Saturday afternoon, second baseman Jose Altuve and third baseman Alex Bregman had messages for him.

"Altuve told me, 'My dad told me this morning that you're gonna be the man of this game and you're gonna win this game today,'" Alvarez recalled in Spanish through an interpreter. "That happened before I came into the clubhouse. He told me that about his dad, and then I walked in, and Bregman said the same thing to me. And then I started getting a little nervous, like, 'Oh, it's my night now?' And that's why I was at peace. Because all these things happened to me to give me all this peace."

Peace reached its peak and morphed into chaos when Alvarez nuked a three-run, 450-foot bomb over the grass-covered batter's eye in center field and put the Astros nine outs away from ensnaring a dream that had dodged them for the last four years.

Alvarez's go-ahead shot all but delivered it, and at the final out he raised both his arms in left field as the Astros claimed their first World Series title since 2017 by beating the Phillies 4-1.

None of his previous 39 home runs this year, in the postseason or regular season, had traveled more than 438 feet. The Astros who bore witness to this one could not recall a ball ever hit that hard, that far, to that spot at Minute Maid Park.

"Guys don't even hit the balls there in BP," pitcher Lance McCullers Jr. said. "We have a short left field and a short right field, but center field here is known as a graveyard. You cannot hit the ball up there physically."

"I've never seen that in my life," Bregman said.

Told later of his teammates' disbelief, Alvarez smiled.

"That's why I was here," he said. "So they could see it."

The dugout began to empty before the ball found its resting place. Alvarez spotted a few teammates who were holdouts, waiting to make sure it was out, and playfully chided them, saying, "What was it? You guys didn't trust that I had enough power to get that out?"

By the time he crossed home plate, a cadre of elated colleagues awaited. Starting pitcher Framber Valdez, who had spun six terrific innings without any run support, stomped his foot. Twelfth-year major league veteran Altuve jumped around like a kid in a bounce house and hung from the arms of two younger teammates.

Alvarez, 25, is the only player in MLB postseason history with multiple career go-ahead home runs in the sixth inning or later with his team trailing. All three of his occurred this year.

Alvarez entered Saturday 2-for-19 with a .385 OPS in the World Series and with just nine hits through Houston's first 12

OPPOSITE: Knowing how to bring a crowd to its feet, Yordan Alvarez obliterated a sixth-inning sinker from Phillies reliever Jose Alvarado, driving it 450 feet with two men aboard to put the Astros up 3-1. That was all the cushion they'd need in clinching the title. JON SHAPLEY/HOUSTON CHRONICLE

postseason games. He had not homered since his game-winning blasts in the first two games of the AL Division Series, deliverances that heroicized him and created expectations he did not meet again for 10 contests. On Saturday against the Phillies, he erased it all with one swing.

The Astros began the bottom of the sixth trailing 1-0 after Kyle Schwarber's home run in the top of the inning. After Martín Maldonado was hit by a Zack Wheeler pitch, Altuve reached on a fielder's choice before Jeremy Peña's one-out single gave the Astros runners at the corners. That prompted Phillies manager Rob Thomson to summon one of his top leverage weapons from the bullpen.

Southpaw José Alvarado held lefthanded hitters to a .322 regular-season slugging percentage and in the regular season and playoffs combined had surrendered just one home run to a lefthanded batter this year. Philadelphia turned to him multiple times in this series to neutralize Alvarez and Kyle Tucker, the two lefties in Houston's lineup. Alvarado plunked Alvarez with the bases loaded in Game 4 to give the Astros a run but had not allowed a hit to the Astros' Cuban slugger in his first three World Series appearances.

As Alvarado warmed up, Alvarez did not rush to review video with his hitting coaches or discuss his approach after going 0-for-2 in his first couple at-bats. He simply watched and waited. When he finally stepped into the batter's box, he said, he was honestly not trying to hit a home run.

"It's about faith for me," he said. "The first two at-bats, I had a plan, and things were not really working out for me. When I saw Peña get that hit and Altuve got to third, in that moment I had peace. I knew that Alvarado was going to come into the game. I knew he was ready for me. I didn't even look at anything. I didn't even go look at the iPad or anything. I waited for my at-bat. I didn't go look at anything because I knew that that was my moment. I had this peace of mind that I knew that that was my moment. And it happened."

Alvarez fouled off the first pitch he saw and watched two more miss the strike zone. Alvarado served a 2-1 sinker over the plate, and Alvarez pounced. Bedlam ensued.

A group of Astros baseball operations staffers watched the game broadcast on delay from a conference room inside the home clubhouse in the bowels of Minute Maid Park. Their only real-time guide was an analytics tool that

OPPOSITE LEFT: With Jeremy Peña right behind him, Jose Altuve heads to the plate thanks to Yordan's Alvarez's first home run since Game 2 of the American League Division Series.
BRETT COOMER/HOUSTON CHRONICLE

OPPOSITE RIGHT: Accepting a low five from third-base coach Gary Pettis was the last thing Alvarez needed to do on his way home.
JON SHAPLEY/HOUSTON CHRONICLE

LEFT: Jim Rice, a lifelong Astros fan who drove from Dallas to see Game 6 after his boss offered him a ticket, wound up with the ball Yordan Alvarez hit for a 450-foot home run. Rice's souvenir traveled over the batter's eye that looms 40 feet above the center-field fence at Minute Maid Park. "I saw it coming right at me," he said, "but I thought there was no way a ball could carry over this wall."
MATT YOUNG/HOUSTON CHRONICLE

depicts players and batted balls as mere dots on a diamond. Before the tiny spot representing Alvarez's homer finished its on-screen flight, they heard roars echoing down the hallway from the field.

McCullers was in what he describes as his "run-scoring position" in the back corner of the trainer's storage room, a superstition born from one fortuitous instance on a day he can no longer recall. On Saturday, he was there when Alvarez answered his prayers.

"He continues to come up for us over and over and over again," McCullers said. "I feel like the three homers he hit this postseason were, like, the biggest homers anyone could ever hit. He's been such an amazing player for us ever since he came here."

Astros center fielder Chas McCormick was one of the last to rush out of the dugout after the home run but defended himself by underscoring its unbelievability.

"I was kind of underneath the tunnel hiding a little bit, and then he hit it, and I was like, 'Holy … ! He crushed that ball,' " McCormick said. "I wanted to make sure. Because center field — no one hits home runs to center field. But he hit it over the backstop. But when he hit it, it was gone. It was awesome to see these guys get out of the dugout like that. Crazy."

Astros hitting coach Alex Cintrón, who helped Alvarez adjust his batting stance before Game 4 against the Phillies, worked with him again in the cage before Saturday's game and came away encouraged by what he saw. Cintrón boasted to the front office that Alvarez would hit a home run that night. Alvarez did not make him into a fool.

After it was all over, after he and his teammates were crowned champions on a confetti-strewn field, Alvarez held his son and daughter in his arms. He would, after all, be free to host his daughter's birthday party at their home Sunday.

The peace he felt earlier before his home run returned. He had no doubt this was how it was all destined to come together.

"It was about the moment," he said. "It was the right moment for that to happen, and that's what I did in the postseason. It was about the right moment."

franklin
HOUSTON
ASTROS
44

Vital to the title

Jeremy Peña named World Series Most Valuable Player

BY MATT YOUNG · NOV. 5, 2022

Jeremy Peña — World Series championship hat flipped backward on his head, gray championship T-shirt turned black and sticky from cheap champagne, and goggles affixed to his forehead — was in mid-dance when someone from the Astros communications staff approached him with a request.

"Whatever you need, big dog, I got you!" the 25-year-old shortstop yelled above the din of music and celebratory yelling in the Minute Maid Park home clubhouse.

Peña was named the World Series Most Valuable Player because of the numerous sparkling defensive plays he made with his solid gold glove and the fact he hit a team-best .400 in the six-game series, capped by the Astros' 4-1 win Saturday night. His "whatever you need, big dog" attitude is what earned him the shouts of approval from his teammates when he was handed the MVP trophy.

"I love that kid. ... Well, he's not a kid anymore. He's a man; he's the man," said Jose Altuve, Peña's double-play partner and the teammate who hit in front of the rookie throughout the playoffs.

After hitting .253 with 22 home runs and playing the best defensive shortstop in the league, which is how he became the first rookie to win a Gold Glove at that position, Peña turned it up several notches in the postseason.

He belted the 18th-inning home run that swept the Mariners out of the American League Division Series. He followed that up by going 6-for-17 (.353) with a pair of home runs in the Astros' sweep of the Yankees. He was named MVP of that American League Championship Series and will be remembered for the Michael Jordanesque shoulder shrug he gave his teammates while rounding third base after a Game 4 home run at Yankee Stadium.

He didn't slow down in the World Series, blasting another home run that came with another shoulder shrug to silence the crowd at raucous Citizens Bank Park in Game 5, then producing a two-hit night in the decisive Game 6.

"Everyone wants to be a big-time player like that, but I just have to give credit to my teammates for putting me in those positions," said Peña, who joins Marlins pitcher Liván Hernández (1997) and Dodgers pitcher Larry Sherry (1959) as the only rookies to be named World Series MVP. "I've just always been so thankful to them for accepting me and helping me with everything along the way and having confidence in me the whole way."

His teammates say Peña had their confidence since spring training, when everyone learned Carlos Correa was headed to Minnesota and Peña was going to be his replacement. It didn't hurt that the rookie showed poise right away and delivered on the field, hitting .281 over his first two months while displaying his stellar defense.

"I think we all noticed how mature he is," Astros ace Justin Verlander said during the clubhouse celebration. "You saw him in all these big spots, right? He never flinched. That's his personality. He's ready for anything and not scared of anything. That's what you want."

Astros manager Dusty Baker showed the ultimate faith in his young guy by putting him second in the lineup late in the season and during the playoffs, sandwiched between All-Stars Altuve and Yordan Alvarez. In the 62 games Peña batted second, regular season and postseason combined, the Astros were a ludicrous 53-9 (.855).

It was in that spot where Peña came through with a big Game 6 hit in the sixth inning. With his team trailing 1-0, he stepped to the plate with one out and Altuve at first after the second baseman had narrowly avoided a double play by hustling down the line. Peña hit a ball up the middle to put runners on the corners for Alvarez, who blasted a ball 450 feet to set the Astros' championship celebration in motion.

"First of all, shout-out to Altuve for beating out the double play," Peña said. "You can't teach hustle. He's hustled all year. He leads by example, and that's something I always look up to.

"It was just pass-the-baton mentality, get on base, and let Yordan do his thing. He's

OPPOSITE: Jeremy Peña put some serious elbow grease into his World Series performance, hitting safely in all six games while going 10-for-25. He wound up producing a .400/.423/.600 slash line with a homer, five runs and three RBIs. **KAREN WARREN/HOUSTON CHRONICLE**

done it all year. He came through for us. That's big-time."

Peña is always quick to deflect credit, but Baker doesn't mind heaping praise on him.

"He deserves everything he gets," Baker said. "He's just incredibly poised. We had faith in him, and he had faith in us. But boy, he came up big, didn't he?"

RIGHT: The first rookie shortstop to win a Gold Glove award, Jeremy Peña unites with double-play partner Jose Altuve, left, in celebration of the Astros' championship. **BRETT COOMER/HOUSTON CHRONICLE**

OPPOSITE: Peña expresses his heartfelt appreciation to Astros fans after being named World Series MVP. The only other rookies to win the honor were Dodgers pitcher Larry Sherry (1959) and Marlins pitcher Liván Hernández (1997). **BRETT COOMER/HOUSTON CHRONICLE**

FOX SPORTS
SERIES
CHAMPIONS
WORLD
CHAMPIONS

WORLD SERIES
WORLD SERIES

Right time, right place

In his 25th year as a major league manager, Dusty Baker gets his championship

BY BRIAN T. SMITH · NOV. 5, 2022

Dusty Baker followed the soaring fireworks and orange confetti, walked onto a field filled with champions, and began hugging everyone he could find.

The 2022 World Series-winning Astros.

His beaming son, Darren.

Friends, fans, longtime admirers and loyal supporters.

In the prouder-than-ever stands of Minute Maid Park, a large sign stood out: "Dusty for President."

Within the same rows filled with orange-and-blue believers, one name was chanted.

"Dusty! Dusty! Dusty!"

It was finally over.

And it was so beautiful.

Baker spent more than a third of his 73 years waiting to win his first World Series as a manager.

Now he and his Astros are undeniable world champions together.

"This town is happy — I mean, everywhere you go. This town, they pull for their teams better than any town I've ever seen. It's wonderful," said Baker, after the Astros downed the Philadelphia Phillies 4-1 in Game 6 and won this Fall Classic 4-2.

For three consecutive seasons and back-to-back World Series in Houston, "Win one for Dusty" echoed throughout the Astros organization.

A come-from-behind win Saturday night before a constantly roaring crowd of 42,958 gave the Astros their second world championship. Once Kyle Tucker gloved the final out, it was pure joy, instant celebration and total release.

"We wanted to sweep. But since we didn't sweep, let's take two out of three (in Philadelphia) and make sure we win it at home," said Baker, wearing large goggles and drenched in champagne inside a pounding clubhouse. "I didn't want to go to Game 7, because Game 6 has been my nemesis. It really has. Game 6, man, I'm like, dang, Game 6 again. But I said my prayers (Friday) night. I said, 'Lord, please don't take us past Game 6 again.' And then when Yordan (Alvarez) hit that ball on the moon out there, man, I said, 'OK, we got action.' "

Both of the Astros' world titles have arrived during a six-year run of American League dominance that has doubled as the greatest era in Houston sports.

An illegal sign-stealing scandal tarnished a 2017 trophy and led to the stunning firings of former skipper A.J. Hinch and general manager Jeff Luhnow on Jan. 13, 2020.

That date, once filled with pain, shame and confusion, has become a positive dividing line three seasons later.

When the Astros franchise was at its lowest point — badly needing image rehabilitation, a new leader on and off the field, and calm daily guidance in the middle of a national firestorm — Baker was there, waiting.

Major League Baseball had moved on from a baseball lifer who was drafted in 1967, hit 242 career home runs, became close friends with Hank Aaron, and won a World Series as an outfielder with the 1981 Los Angeles Dodgers. Baker's professional life kept changing and being challenged as he managed San Francisco with Barry Bonds, Chicago with Sammy Sosa, Cincinnati with Joey Votto, and Washington with Bryce Harper before being forced to the side.

The Astros needed serious help and a wise, trusted hand.

But who would want the job and willingly enter the fury?

Baker, who thought he might never manage again.

"I'm extremely thankful for this opportunity," Baker said in January 2020. "This is a great ballclub with outstanding players that know how to win. I applaud (Astros owner) Jim Crane for the leadership he has shown in recent weeks and look forward to working with him and the players to bring a championship to the city of Houston."

The first spring training was a media nightmare.

Then the coronavirus pandemic hit, and Baker went 29-31 during a severely shortened regular season. Those Astros made the playoffs only because of an expanded postseason field.

Hinch often had a perfect touch with the

OPPOSITE: With trademark toothpick in place after a monstrous home run by Yordan Alvarez put the Astros up 3-1 in Game 6, Dusty Baker could practically taste his first championship as a manager.
KAREN WARREN/HOUSTON CHRONICLE

RIGHT: Dusty Baker, right, initiates a squeeze play with Astros reliever Héctor Neris after becoming, at 73, the oldest MLB manager to take a team to a championship. Jack McKeon was 72 when he piloted the Marlins to the 2003 crown.
BRETT COOMER/HOUSTON CHRONICLE

rebuilt Astros, who won it all in 2017 and united a city after the destruction from Hurricane Harvey.

Was Baker the right skipper for a remade team that would, by the time pandemic restrictions were lifted, be viciously booed from ballpark to ballpark across America?

The Astros' final three weeks of their 2020 season said everything about Baker and his connection with a club that traded outside hate for inner togetherness and huge victories.

A veteran manager, once shredded for his inability to handle pitching staffs and adapt to the rise of the analytics age, kept getting the best out of the new Astros. They reached Game 7 of the 2020 AL Championship Series, fell short, then never looked back.

Last year's Astros won 95 games and hosted Game 1 of that Fall Classic before falling to Atlanta. Baker, facing an uncertain future and managing for another contract, embraced the life evolution that can come with temporary pain. He vowed, "We'll be back," before walking off a stage and heading into a darkened hallway.

"What can you do?" Baker said on Nov. 2, 2021. "Except go home, take a shower, figure out how you're going to come back and win it next year."

One day, Baker will be enshrined in the National Baseball Hall of Fame. His life deserves a movie. With every game, there's always a new story, an old song or a bygone name that he goes out of his way to pay tribute to.

"This is my third try," Baker said. "I was talking to Tommy (Lasorda on Saturday) after the game. … I talked to my dad and Hank. I said last year was the Braves' year — that was Hank Aaron's year, the year he died. And this is the 75th year of Jackie Robinson, and it's the first year for me."

A manager with 2,093 regular-season victories and 51 playoff wins also saw 20 years of personal and professional growth in his

LEFT: The third time was a charm for Dusty Baker, who'd lost his previous two World Series appearances as a manager with the 2002 Giants and 2021 Astros. Houston's 11-2 run through the playoffs left Baker with 51 postseason victories, fourth all-time behind Joe Torre (84), Tony La Russa (71) and Bobby Cox (67). **BRETT COOMER/HOUSTON CHRONICLE**

son, who once had to be pulled away from home plate while his father was on the verge of winning a 2002 world championship that ended up one win away.

"Twenty years ago, (Darren) was 3 years old and a batboy," Baker said. "I think highly of my son, and he's probably the most positive person that I've met. He's no longer a kid, but you know how kids are. I mean, you go fishing, they're always thinking they're going to catch something, and he does. And he reminds me that, 'Hey, Dad, you know, you'll get it done.' "

As Baker bounced from live TV postgame set to live TV postgame set Saturday night, pointing toward all the fans screaming his first name, Darren watched and waited.

Then a son wearing a throwback Astros cap hugged a father wearing a new "World Series champions 2022" Astros cap.

"It's hard for me to believe," Darren said. "I know everything he's been through, ups and downs. This means everything."

Baker kept chewing on his trademark toothpick and staring out at the green grass and red dirt as the innings mounted in Game 6. His team finally broke through in the bottom of the sixth. Alvarez magically changed everything with a 450-foot monster shot to deep center field. "We want Houston" chants proudly poured from the stands. Alvarez walked to the end of the home dugout to high-five his leader.

What happened the second that the final out became a life-changing world championship?

"My coaching staff mobbed me in the dugout," Baker said. "I had to hold on to the fence. I was mobbed. But I didn't care."

Baker led Houston's Astros to a world title that answered everything and should silence any remaining haters.

After waiting decades for his first championship as a manager, the 73-year-old baseball lifer finally won the World Series with the team that was perfect for him.

Their second World Series championship made the Astros the fifth team in the 2000s with multiple titles, joining the Red Sox (four), Giants (three), Yankees (two) and Cardinals (two). **BRETT COOMER/HOUSTON CHRONICLE**

With all hands on deck, first baseman Yuli Gurriel hoists the Commissioner's Trophy during the Astros' postgame celebration. Gurriel, who was unable to play in the World Series clincher because of an MCL sprain suffered in Game 5, is flanked by Jose Altuve, left, Christian Vázquez, right, and Chas McCormick, far right. BRETT COOMER/HOUSTON CHRONICLE

ASTROS
SHERIFF
Bell

PARADE

Ode to joy

Astros celebration in downtown Houston brings out the adoring masses

BY BRIAN T. SMITH · NOV. 7, 2022

A young boy improved his positioning in the middle of a tree, holding up a cellphone while staring down an overloaded downtown Houston street that would soon be filled with World Series champions.

Behind the boy in the tree, four kids climbed a metal barrier and attempted to move higher. A child wearing a bright orange No. 27 Jose Altuve jersey moved up a couple more rows, then settled in for the long parade.

Impromptu chants began two hours before a "3, 2, 1" crowd countdown promptly led into noon Monday, two days after the Astros started a citywide party that hasn't stopped.

"We want Houston!"

"You got Houston!"

"We want Houston!"

"You got Houston!"

So this is what it's like when you finally win the whole darn thing in 2017, remove the shine from a once-perfect trophy, then win the whole darn thing again in 2022 and finally silence the national haters.

Local perfection, take two.

Helicopters and drones hovered above packed-together believers.

An oversized baseball waited for its unveiling in a heart-pounding baseball town.

Interstates backed up at 8:30 a.m., not because of normal Houston traffic but because of all the endless Astros fans.

"It's very city strong. You can't explain it, man. It's what it is. We love our team, and it's very united," said Stephen Saldana, a 30-year-old electrical contractor who was born and raised in Houston and sported a No. 2 Alex Bregman Space City jersey Monday.

A "Y'all Still Mad?" sign was carried through downtown streets on what would normally have been a work/school day.

Standing near the sign: someone wearing a full astronaut costume and carrying a horn.

By 12:45 p.m., marching bands were blasting, huge trucks were rolling, and the name that filled Minute Maid Park after a brilliant Game 6 of the 2022 Fall Classic was again shouted everywhere.

"Dusty! Dusty! Dusty!"

A 73-year-old World Series-winning manager waved and waved, sharing a float with Lance McCullers Jr. and Altuve while a shining trophy was displayed nearby.

Three hours before a rolling stage with "World Series Champions" prominently attached to the back wheeled across Congress Street and slowly carved a path down Smith Street, Yolle Lemberger put the finishing touches on his contributions to a parade that marked another high point during the greatest era in Astros history.

"The Astros are going to be on the floats I touched," said Lemberger, who moved to Houston in 1992 and runs Yak Werks with his wife. "Until half an hour ago, I built everything, painted, decorated. I'm tweaking (them) right now."

Craig Biggio and Jeff Bagwell shared the same large truck.

The University of Houston and Texas Southern were loudly represented, while NASA also played a part.

Tight snare rolls and a piercing whistle followed the ringing "3, 2, 1" countdown. Then the boom, boom, boom from big bass drums.

When's the last time Phil Maton was rabidly cheered? The Astros reliever was celebrated Monday with an "I love you, Phil!" scream.

Mauricio Dubón received the same world champion treatment on a day devoted to the best year in Astros history.

A regular season with 106 wins. An unbelievable postseason with 11 more as the Astros erased the Seattle Mariners, New York Yankees and Philadelphia Phillies.

Ryan Pressly and Jeremy Peña rode together after the final win inside Minute Maid Park. A handmade heart sign, of course, followed the World Series and American League Championship Series MVP everywhere.

David Hensley rolled by.

OPPOSITE: Cheers from above and below engulfed the Astros as they traversed the streets of downtown Houston for a victory parade two days after winning the 2022 World Series. **BRETT COOMER/HOUSTON CHRONICLE**

FOLLOWING LEFT: Yordan Alvarez, who did a lot of heavy lifting for the Astros' offense in 2022, had no problem whatsoever with the Commissioner's Trophy. **YI-CHIN LEE/HOUSTON CHRONICLE**

FOLLOWING MIDDLE: The Astros' boom times are something to savor for Framber Valdez, flanked by fellow pitchers Héctor Neris, left, and Cristian Javier. And as usual, closer Ryan Pressly has their backs. **BRETT COOMER/HOUSTON CHRONICLE**

FOLLOWING RIGHT: On a beautiful day in Houston, local radar detected only scattered confetti showers. **JASON FOCHTMAN/HOUSTON CHRONICLE**

"Hensley!" was immediately shouted.

Yordan Alvarez and Chas McCormick, together, were hailed as conquering heroes days after Alvarez changed an entire season with 450 feet of instant magic and McCormick left an outfield impression inside Citizens Bank Park that will never be forgotten.

Orange towels, thrown from trucks and floats, were begged for. One fell short on the street. A police officer picked it up and handed the 2022 treasure to a thankful fan.

The screams kept echoing.

"Astros! Astros! Astros!" became the latest chant.

Then the last championship chariot disappeared.

Scattered pieces of blue confetti were still falling from the sky when a fan, wearing a Kyle Tucker No. 30 jersey and carrying a large orange flag, began walking by Buffalo Bayou.

More fans wearing Astros orange jerseys sprinted past on bicycles, following the same flowing water.

Unlike 2017, this championship should sparkle forever.

On Monday in downtown Houston, children and adults climbed trees, pressed against barriers and waited for hours just to get as close as possible to all the Astros who won Houston a World Series again.

600
Lamar
PEÑA
3
55
50
WORLD SERIES
CHAMPIONS
POLICE
HOUSTON POLICE

Regular season · batting stats

Name	AB	R	H	HR	RBI	BB	SO	SB	AVG	OBP	SLG	OPS
Alex Bregman 3B	548	93	142	23	93	87	77	1	.259	.366	.454	.820
Yuli Gurriel 1B	545	53	132	8	53	30	73	8	.242	.288	.360	.647
Kyle Tucker RF	544	71	140	30	107	59	95	25	.257	.330	.478	.808
Jose Altuve 2B	527	103	158	28	57	66	87	18	.300	.387	.533	.921
Jeremy Peña SS	521	72	132	22	63	22	135	11	.253	.289	.426	.715
Yordan Alvarez LF	470	95	144	37	97	78	106	1	.306	.406	.613	1.019
Chas McCormick CF	359	47	88	14	44	46	106	4	.245	.332	.407	.738
Martín Maldonado C	344	40	64	15	45	22	116	0	.186	.248	.352	.600
Aledmys Díaz IF	305	35	74	12	38	18	53	1	.243	.287	.403	.691
Michael Brantley LF	243	28	70	5	26	31	30	1	.288	.370	.416	.785
Mauricio Dubón CF	197	21	41	3	16	12	26	2	.208	.254	.294	.548
Trey Mancini DH	165	17	29	8	22	18	49	0	.176	.258	.364	.622
Jake Meyers CF	150	13	34	1	15	7	54	2	.227	.269	.313	.582
Jose Siri CF	135	18	24	3	10	9	48	6	.178	.238	.304	.542
Christian Vázquez C	104	8	26	1	10	4	18	0	.250	.278	.308	.585
Jason Castro C	78	6	9	1	3	8	40	1	.115	.205	.179	.384
J.J. Matijevic 1B	67	7	14	2	5	2	25	1	.209	.254	.328	.582
Niko Goodrum 2B	43	2	5	0	1	2	23	1	.116	.156	.163	.318
David Hensley DH	29	7	10	1	5	5	6	0	.345	.441	.586	1.027
Korey Lee C	25	1	4	0	4	1	9	0	.160	.192	.240	.432
Yainer Diaz C	8	0	1	0	1	1	2	0	.125	.222	.250	.472
Joe Perez 3B	1	0	0	0	0	0	1	0	.000	.000	.000	.000
Taylor Jones 1B	1	0	0	0	0	0	0	0	.000	.000	.000	.000

Source: espn.com

Regular season · pitching stats

Name	GP	W	L	SV	HLD	IP	H	ER	HR	BB	K	WHIP	ERA
Framber Valdez LHP	31	17	6	0	0	201.1	166	63	11	67	194	1.16	2.82
Justin Verlander RHP	28	18	4	0	0	175	116	34	12	29	185	0.83	1.75
José Urquidy RHP	29	13	8	0	0	164.1	154	72	29	38	134	1.17	3.94
Luis Garcia RHP	28	15	8	0	0	157.1	131	65	23	47	157	1.13	3.72
Cristian Javier RHP	30	11	9	0	1	148.2	89	42	17	52	194	0.95	2.54
Rafael Montero RHP	71	5	2	14	23	68.1	47	18	3	23	73	1.02	2.37
Phil Maton RHP	67	0	2	0	14	65.2	58	28	10	24	73	1.25	3.84
Héctor Neris RHP	70	6	4	3	25	65.1	49	27	3	17	79	1.01	3.72
Bryan Abreu RHP	55	4	0	2	8	60.1	45	13	2	26	88	1.18	1.94
Jake Odorizzi RHP	12	4	3	0	0	60	52	25	5	17	46	1.15	3.75
Ryne Stanek RHP	59	2	1	1	17	54.2	36	7	2	31	62	1.23	1.15
Ryan Pressly RHP	50	3	3	33	0	48.1	30	16	4	13	65	0.89	2.98
Lance McCullers Jr. RHP	8	4	2	0	0	47.2	37	12	4	22	50	1.24	2.27
Seth Martinez RHP	29	1	1	0	3	38.2	26	9	3	14	38	1.03	2.09
Will Smith LHP	24	0	2	0	6	22	23	8	2	4	24	1.23	3.27
Hunter Brown RHP	7	2	0	0	2	20.1	15	2	0	7	22	1.08	0.89
Blake Taylor LHP	19	1	1	0	4	16	15	7	1	10	9	1.56	3.94
Brandon Bielak RHP	5	0	0	0	1	12.1	11	5	2	4	12	1.22	3.65
Parker Mushinski LHP	7	0	0	0	1	7.1	5	3	0	3	8	1.09	3.68
Ronel Blanco RHP	7	0	0	0	0	6.1	8	5	1	4	7	1.89	7.11
Enoli Paredes RHP	3	0	0	0	0	3	3	1	0	3	2	2.00	3.00
Pedro Báez RHP	3	0	0	0	0	2.1	5	3	0	3	2	3.43	11.57

Postseason · batting stats

Name	AB	R	H	HR	RBI	BB	SO	SB	AVG	OBP	SLG	OPS
Jose Altuve 2B	58	8	11	0	0	4	14	1	.190	.242	.241	.483
Jeremy Peña SS	58	12	20	4	8	2	15	0	.345	.367	.638	1.005
Yordan Alvarez LF	52	9	10	3	14	6	16	0	.192	.311	.423	.735
Alex Bregman 3B	51	7	15	3	11	6	6	1	.294	.379	.569	.948
Kyle Tucker RF	49	4	10	3	6	7	14	1	.204	.298	.408	.706
Yuli Gurriel 1B	49	4	17	2	4	1	1	2	.347	.360	.490	.850
Chas McCormick CF	39	5	9	2	3	5	15	0	.231	.333	.385	.718
Martín Maldonado C	29	2	6	0	2	2	11	0	.207	.303	.241	.544
Aledmys Díaz LF	22	0	1	0	0	0	6	0	.045	.087	.091	.178
Trey Mancini DH	21	0	1	0	1	1	8	0	.048	.125	.048	.173
Christian Vázquez C	17	1	4	0	3	1	6	0	.235	.316	.235	.551
David Hensley DH	8	0	2	0	0	0	4	0	.250	.333	.250	.583
Jake Meyers CF	2	1	0	0	0	0	2	0	.000	.000	.000	.000

Postseason · pitching stats

Name	GP	W	L	SV	HLD	IP	H	ER	HR	BB	K	WHIP	ERA
Framber Valdez LHP	4	3	0	0	0	25	14	4	1	8	33	0.88	1.44
Justin Verlander RHP	4	2	0	0	0	20	23	13	3	8	25	1.55	5.85
Lance McCullers Jr. RHP	3	0	1	0	0	15.1	16	10	5	4	18	1.30	5.87
Cristian Javier RHP	3	2	0	0	0	12.2	2	1	1	5	16	0.55	0.71
Bryan Abreu RHP	10	0	0	0	5	11.1	4	0	0	4	19	0.71	0.00
Ryan Pressly RHP	10	0	0	6	0	11	4	0	0	3	13	0.64	0.00
Rafael Montero RHP	10	1	0	0	4	9.1	5	2	1	6	10	1.18	1.93
Héctor Neris RHP	8	2	0	0	3	6	2	1	1	0	9	0.33	1.50
Luis Garcia RHP	2	1	1	0	0	5.2	4	1	1	0	6	0.71	1.59
Hunter Brown RHP	3	0	0	0	0	3.2	2	0	0	3	1	1.36	0.00
Ryne Stanek RHP	4	0	0	0	0	3	0	0	0	1	6	0.33	0.00
José Urquidy RHP	1	0	0	0	0	3	1	0	0	1	4	0.67	0.00